Late Heaney

Late He

Late Heaney

NICHOLAS ALLEN

OXFORD
UNIVERSITY PRESS

Great Clarendon Street, Oxford, OX2 6DP,
United Kingdom

Oxford University Press is a department of the University of Oxford.
It furthers the University's objective of excellence in research, scholarship,
and education by publishing worldwide. Oxford is a registered trade mark of
Oxford University Press in the UK and in certain other countries.

© Nicholas Allen 2026

The moral rights of the author have been asserted.

All rights reserved. No part of this publication may be reproduced, stored in a retrieval system,
transmitted, used for text and data mining, or used for training artificial intelligence, in any form or
by any means, without the prior permission in writing of Oxford University Press, or as expressly
permitted by law, by licence or under terms agreed with the appropriate reprographics rights
organization. Enquiries concerning reproduction outside the scope of the above should be sent
to the Rights Department, Oxford University Press, at the address above.

You must not circulate this work in any other form
and you must impose this same condition on any acquirer.

Published in the United States of America by Oxford University Press
198 Madison Avenue, New York, NY 10016, United States of America

British Library Cataloguing in Publication Data
Data available

Library of Congress Control Number: 2025941937

ISBN 9780198985402

DOI: 10.1093/9780198985419.001.0001

The manufacturer's authorised representative in the EU for product safety is
Oxford University Press España S.A. of Parque Empresarial San Fernando de Henares,
Avenida de Castilla, 2 – 28830 Madrid (www.oup.es/en or product.safety@oup.com).
OUP España S.A. also acts as importer into Spain of products made by the manufacturer.

Links to third party websites are provided by Oxford in good faith and
for information only. Oxford disclaims any responsibility for the materials
contained in any third party website referenced in this work.

For Louise, and for my friends

To find my home in one sentence, concise, as if hammered in metal.

Czeslaw Milosz

Acknowledgements

I am grateful to the many people who helped me in the research and writing of this book. Thank you to my anonymous readers, and to everyone at Oxford University Press. Marie, Catherine, and Christopher Heaney have been both generous and welcoming; I hope the book speaks true to them. Thanks especially to George and Anne Allen, Nigel, James and Muriel Allen, John Brannigan, Bob Carson, Colin Davidson, Blair Dorminey, Neil Hegarty, Tony DeMarco, Bertis Downs, Martin Doyle, Martin Fanning, John Kerrigan, Jane and Barry Kidney, David Lloyd, Dave Marr, James McCreight, Andrew McNeillie, Jacqueline Norton, Iarla Ó Lionáird, Eve Patten, Kathy Prescott and Grady Thrasher, David Prout, John Purser, Alan Riach, John and Jane Robertson, Fiona Stafford, Winnie Smith, and Mary Shine Thompson. As always, all of this would be as nothing without Louise, Chloe, Patrick, and Cormac, the watermark in these pages.

Quotations from Seamus Heaney's work are reproduced by permission of the Estate of Seamus Heaney, and of Faber and Faber, and Farrar, Straus and Giroux. The quotation in the epigraph from Czeslaw Milosz is reproduced by permission of HarperCollins.

The cover image is a lithograph of Seamus Heaney by Colin Davidson (2013).

Contents

Note on the Text   xiii
Foreword   xv

1. Stockholm in Pylos   1
2. Landscapes   21
3. Bearings   54
4. Ghosts   82
5. The Riverbank Fields   108
   Afterword   131

Further Reading   137
Title Index   143
General Index   145

Note on the Text

For ease of reference, I have assumed all poems are by Heaney unless indicated otherwise in the text or notes. To avoid repetition, I have used the following abbreviations for book titles: *Death of a Naturalist* (DN); *Door into the Dark* (DD); *Wintering Out* (WO); *North* (N); *Field Work* (FW); *The Cure at Troy* (CAT); *Sweeney Astray* (SA); *Station Island* (SI); *The Haw Lantern* (HL); *Seeing Things* (ST); Nobel Lecture (NL); *The Spirit Level* (SL); *Electric Light* (EL); *District and Circle* (DC); *Human Chain* (HC); *Finders Keepers* (FK); *Stepping Stones* (SS); *Aeneid: Book VI* (AVI); and *The Letters of Seamus Heaney* (LSH).

Foreword

Seamus Heaney lived nearly all of his writing life in public view. He published his first collection in 1966 with Faber when he was in his mid-twenties and his last in 2010, three years before he died in 2013. By then, he was a Nobel Laureate, a national figure on the island of Ireland and the symbol for many of a literary tradition whose fellows are Yeats, Joyce, and Beckett. These lineages quickly date, as is certainly true of Heaney, who was first read as a nature poet in the mode of Ted Hughes before being cast as a northern writer framed by the latest phase of a century of Irish troubles. Both perspectives show a partial truth, but art has always the capacity to exceed its circumstances. Sometimes this happens in a poem that seems to have come from nowhere. At others, the right word or phrase emerges as the consequence of a lifetime's waiting and working. Heaney experienced both kinds of arrival, usually in one of the quiet places he needed to write. Heaney associated poetry with solitude and withdrawal into a place of refuge, such as he imagined Glanmore cottage in Wicklow and later his attic office in Sandymount, by the sea. Withdrawn, he wrote poems that shed light on landscapes of memory that opened out as he aged, making familiar places new in a natural extension of a poetry he had spent decades working over.

As a public poet, Heaney has been the subject of thousands of essays, reviews, interviews, and books. Why then write another one now? Firstly, there is much more written about the poetry he published before he won the Nobel Prize in 1995 than there is after it. Secondly, that later poetry makes a journey that rewards closer reading, principally because it maps his literary experience of aging and illness. This experience gave Heaney's work after the Nobel a different form and context, a deepening and a departure that gives this book its name, a lateness that becomes a style. *Late Heaney* follows the poet through the landscapes, communities, and artists that he wrote about in *The Spirit Level, Electric Light, District and Circle,* and *Human Chain*, coming in the end to a literary geography that is to the water meadows of Lough Neagh as Wordsworth's poetry is to Grasmere.

The book begins with this foreword to situate Heaney as a writer and to introduce myself as a reader. Next there is a chapter on Heaney's travels from Greece, where he learned he had been awarded the Nobel, to Stockholm, where he accepted it. This gives some sense of what this time meant for him, and for his writing, and is an opportunity to share in his sense of self-reflection as he looked back over his career and his life. I take the moment of the Nobel to be the beginning of the late phase because it is a clear point of transition in his writing and in his life. For this reason, *Late Heaney* focuses on those four poetry collections he published after 1995 as its subject. There follow three chapters on the places, people, and memories that shape Heaney's work in this final period. These include descriptions of the landscapes he lived in and imagined, and readings of his translations, each of which is a small act of crossing between a known world and another. The book closes with a consideration of Heaney's late work from the perspective of the riverbank, a place that features powerfully in his final poems, resonant as it is with images of death, and a brief afterword that reflects on Heaney's poetic afterlife. For all that, this is, surprisingly, a book of the light more than dark, Heaney's poems dedicated to the practice of illumination.

As with all literature, the conditions for reading Heaney continue to change, and a poetry that speaks of peace and reconciliation seems at odds with our burning world. Perhaps it has always been, except now that climate change has given authoritarianism and war the added appearance of the inescapable, which only gives aid to tyranny. Heaney was familiar with the problem of fatedness. It haunted him through the Troubles, in his reading of the Trojan War and in his translation of *Beowulf*. The shelter of the hall often felt like a thin line between community and disaster, as conditions in his home place so often proved. In retrospect, his poetry was a lifelong act of learning, adjusting to time and circumstance as best it could. As such, it proceeded from roots that were sunk deep in Heaney's consciousness, his idea of enlightenment growing from the gleam of a farmyard pump to spill into the summer evenings of the last poems, 'the big lift'[1] of the riverbank framed by the sky. This book follows that journey in the period from Heaney's win-

[1] 'The Harvest Bow', *FW*.

ning the Nobel until the publication of his last collection. The portrait that emerges is of a late poetry populated by people and places long held in mind, the poet become a ghost of himself in a landscape worn so thin as to become transcendent.

For my own part, *Late Heaney* pays a small gift of attention in return for the poems, which are my old familiars, as is the landscape in which many of them are set, which has gathered over the decades like river silt. Together this is braided through with years of deep reading and thinking, and seen, perhaps, through a lens that brings some of Heaney's own experiences to bear, my life in Belfast, Dublin, and the United States an echo of the poet's transits. I read Heaney early at school when he was well-known, but nothing of the major figure he became later, and I read him still. In that Belfast of the early eighties Frank Ormsby, a poet himself and then editor of the *Honest Ulsterman*, would cut out and photocopy poems by Heaney, Ciaran Carson, Paul Muldoon, and others for English classes at the Royal Belfast Academical Institution. Ormsby was a volcanic figure, roaring in fury if something stupid was said, as was often the case, according to his lights. He was also bright and fearless and believed we should read work spoken in voices not far from our own, exploring familiar places, which were worthy of description. This was no small thing at a time when the evidence of everyday life was unrelentingly grim. Even the images of it were disconcerting. I remember vividly as a young child watching the evening news from London, which showed thousands of mourners following the coffin of Bobby Sands. The procession was a few miles from my house but seemed a universe away from the quiet suburbs of East Belfast. I had no words for that distance then, and sometimes do not now, but the awareness of the depth of the dissociation between time, place, and event was an early register of the distortions we lived in. Violence was not simply an act of physical aggression, with definite origins and effects. It was a function of the society in all its expressions, soaked through like a watermark. Perhaps this is why so much of the literature from that time and after is written in the fog and rain, permeability a register of the trauma we inhabited, however we cared to recognize it, or not.

Certainly, this sense of disturbance was a bridge for me between the rural and remote world of Heaney's poetry and the Belfast I knew. Early on, I inclined to Paul Muldoon and the wildness of a poem like 'Gathering Mushrooms', which had all the local grit with something of the otherworldly. I read that combination in a Heaney poem like 'North', and for years that series of three books in the seventies had all my attention. *Wintering Out, North,* and *Field Work* are books of a time and place that is very remote from contemporary Ireland, even if the aftermath of that period is still there like a distant Atlantic thundering. The three books fit together in ways that were not apparent to Heaney as he wrote them. He worried about *Wintering Out* in particular, exhausted as he was by the business of making a living as a writer, bringing up a family, and moving to the uncertain quarters of Glanmore before they settled in Sandymount. The stress put a warp in the work, which Heaney worked into an arc that stretched from his home place around Bellaghy to other cultures whose literature resonated with him, to the further north of Scandinavia, the warm south through Dante's Florence to Virgil's Rome, to Poland, and frequently, the Americas. I write arc because it suggests the lift and descent of flight, an elevation that Heaney often invoked in his poems, and because it speaks to the thin form of a line whose skyward transit invites the reader to look up, above. This is one point of connection between the early poetry and the later, which is so much invested in air, sunlight, cloud, and space. These were not just matters of natural effect for Heaney but the aesthetic consequence of his processing years of experience into his poetry. The late light is Heaney's personal, reading and social history filtered through the imagery of place and time. It is a filter and a clarification, and sometimes a warmth. It is a gesture too to what comes after, an illumination that might outlive its source, 'love...sunk past its gleam'.[2]

Not that there was much light then to go round. Heaney looked for it first in captured forms, in the bleb of icicles and the burnt rock of meteorite. This seemed truer to the moment, stuck as we were in a repetitive deadening of atrocity and language. Small things seemed our lot. That horizon remained fixed in my undergraduate education at Queen's University Belfast, where we were dosed on Louis MacNeice, W. H. Auden, and Keith Douglas. We read the war poets without

---

[2] 'Mossbawn: Two Poems in Dedication', *N*.

discussing the fact that we lived in one. The Troubles were a matter for regret elsewhere, a fiction that made discussion of the books we read a discovery of subtext and implication. As readers, we were tuned into alternate and subterranean frequencies, which echoed in the music we listened to and the pubs and parties we frequented. Everything was underground, stashed for a future we had no vocabulary for. It took a special kind of empathy to see the deep feeling in our manic detachments, as happened when Michael Allen brought me to his eyrie office in the English Department and read through my essays as he ate his white bread sandwiches, minding his crumbs into the Tupperware. Michael had come to Belfast in 1965 and was a member of the famous 'Belfast Group' that nurtured so many writers, his friend Heaney among them. His owlish look was patient and precise, his soft English accent with not a trace of the condescension we sometimes otherwise faced. I remember him here as one of Heaney's close and careful readers, and as someone who helped me understand Heaney's own hard-won freedom as a practice, not an end.[3]

It takes dedication to art and to the self to keep going, after all the awards and accolades. It might even be a kind of compulsion given the toll it takes on the mind and body, on friends and family too. The published letters mark this clearly. They show too how carefully Heaney had to manage his public profile in a culture that could be jealous and unkind. His affability was natural, but also protective, a geniality that created the impression of intimacy without giving way to closeness. Still, by the time he won the Nobel Prize, his words had become part of the imaginary fabric of the north at a time when its peace process finally stopped the mass, monotonous killing. Heaney did not think his poetry had helped bring this partial resolution about. At most, he felt it sustained a place for thought that if destroyed would give way to a reduction in our sense of the world that would prepare for absolute hopelessness. Later in his life and after his stroke, he felt some of this despair. But by then, he had a new language to mediate it, one that had moved beyond the old images of earth and touch to an immanent

---

[3] For a sense of Michael Allen's influence on poetry from the north of Ireland, read Fran Brearton's edition of his essays, *Close Readings* (Irish Academic Press, 2015).

architecture of light and sensation. Heaney did in the end what no other writer of his place and time could, which was to raise the underground to the overworld, making light of the shades until they lost their haunting purchase. This was, in its way, a new beginning, mindful of the past but not bound by it. The desire can be read in many of Heaney's poems of the period around the Nobel and the Good Friday Agreement, particularly in those that break down the moment into its molecular patterns, as if a bomb might be made diffuse.

Heaney understood the difficult circuitry of his cultural moment, always aware of what he called Ireland's 'sensitive acoustics'.[4] His quiet mastery of the orchestra was soon tested on a major scale with his award of the Nobel, which is another reason to start with that moment as the point of transition between his earlier and his later work. Lateness then is a condition of time, and of experience, both of which influenced the poetry in ways that made it different in shape and volume from what had gone before.[5] Reading Heaney like this brings aspects of the poetry into a better light than might be the case if reading had continued to recognize and repeat that which is more familiar. Put simply, Heaney began to look up after years of looking down, and in doing so, he animated the poems with a light whose points of origin were in deep time, and meant to last. There is a fitting image for this in the days after he learned he had won the Nobel, swept away from Pylos to Athens by helicopter and the public world of interviews, congratulations, and constant recognition, which he never escaped again.

Late Heaney owes much to the many brilliant readers of his work, especially those who have written about the places that Heaney loved and that surface also in the following pages. A selection of these accounts can be found at the end of the book as suggestions for further reading. For now, we begin with Heaney in Greece, unaware for the moment of

---

[4] To Ann Saddlemyer, 24 January 1972, *LSH*.
[5] Perhaps the most resonant critical formation of the idea of lateness in an artist's work was described by Edward Said, who articulated two possibilities in the term. In one, 'late works crown a lifetime of aesthetic endeavour'. In the other is the 'angry and disturbed artist' who explores 'the experience of late style' as 'a nonharmonious, nonserene tension'. Edward Said, *On Late Style: Music and Literature against the Grain* (Pantheon, 2006), 7. I find Heaney's late work to be neither linear nor fragmentary. Instead, I have tended to use lateness as an image of time and illumination, the later writing a refrain of adjusting forms.

the excitement at home and the beginning of his new life, unbidden. His welcome in Stockholm gave Heaney a chance to reflect on the moment as arrival and departure, awake to the new world like Telemachos, in search of direction. *Late Heaney* follows the way that he went, by riverbank and field, in company of presences we might know as ghosts if the poet had not already banished the dark. This was Heaney's last work, and his greatest, his world remade a final time in the after-image of all that had gone before.

1
Stockholm in Pylos

October in Pylos, the light of the sun on sand, the landscape layered with histories as old as poetry. The journey there by road, westerly from Athens, took the Heaneys through Arcadia, Sparta, and Mycenae, with their friends, Dimitri and Cynthia Hadzi. The trip joined many parts of Heaney's life: an interest in the classical world, good company, fields, rivers, and a playful sense of arrival, as when he recited a few lines from *The Cure at Troy* at the ancient theatre of Epidaurus. A little north are the remains of Agamemnon's palace, from where you can see the blue inlet from which the ships sailed for Troy. Heaney thought of that place when he imagined what peace might look like in Ireland. Worn down by war, and burdened with the premonition of lasting trauma, 'The Mycenae Lookout' kept watch, as the poet had, for signs of better days to come. The late century invited hope for the future, the dying years of the Northern Troubles yielding to ceasefire and peace talks, the intractable giving way to the imaginative. The richness of the landscape fitted this moment, Kalamata drowsy in the autumn heat, Pylos a haven after days in the car on swerving mountain roads. The Peloponnesian coast is the outer rim of a bowl of olive trees, which grow to the outskirts of the port of Kalamata, ringed now by new roads that soon peter out in the Mani, the Greek Connemara. Heaney had been immersed imaginatively in this landscape for years. He read widely in classical literature and was attentive by nature and experience to the countryside they drove through, ordered as it was by agricultural rhythms long familiar to him.

Pylos was familiar to Heaney too. In ancient times it was home to Nestor, the king and elder. Nestor's advice to the young Telemachos gave the prince fortitude to continue in the *Odyssey*, a theme that Heaney took up when overwhelmed by the news that he had won the Nobel

2 LATE HEANEY

Prize for Literature, which he discovered two days after his family when he phoned home to Dublin. Dimitri Hadzi remembered shrieks from the balcony, champagne, and a quiet, reflective dinner, which came to life when the restaurant owner discovered the identity of his guests. Heaney caught the moment differently later in 'Sonnets from Hellas', the sequence he wrote to commemorate this transformative time in his life. The admonishment to be more himself was one Heaney took to heart, and a theme he returned to again in his Nobel speech. It is the kind of plain speaking that can be shallow if the mouth that shapes it is not accustomed to silence. In this case Heaney carried within himself the depth of deathly decades, which didn't end with his award of the Nobel. He was conscious of this as he imagined the line between self and poetry as a music that unstrung violence. It was an imperfect equation, and a continuing journey, which overshadowed his return to Greece two years later:

> ...it was there in Olympia, down among green willows,
> The lustral wash and run of river shallows,
> That we heard of Sean Brown's murder in the grounds
> Of Bellaghy GAA Club. And imagined
> Hose-water smashing hard back off the asphalt
> In the car park where his athlete's blood ran cold.[1]

Among all the deaths, I remember this one with particular melancholy.[2] My family had moved from Belfast to Magherafelt in County Derry with my father's job some years before and the intimacy between terror and the townlands was disturbingly close in those late years of the Troubles. On the road from Magherafelt, Bellaghy is a dip in the road from Castledawson to Portglenone, shelving off on one side to the shores of Lough Neagh, shouldered on the other by the rising ground of the Sperrins. The GAA club is off to the right of the crossroads, down a

---

[1] 'Sonnets from Hellas', EL.
[2] Sean Brown was murdered on 12 May 1997. His killers have not been prosecuted. Similar is true of several other individuals that Heaney wrote elegies for. No one has been held accountable for the murders of Sean Armstrong ('A Postcard from North Antrim'), Colum McCartney ('The Strand at Lough Beg'), or Louis O'Neill ('Casualty').

country road that narrows towards the outflow of the River Bann. Heaney later described the landscape around here as veiled, and the image is well chosen. Bleak in winter and early Spring, it is luminous in the May and June time, the ditches threaded with hazel and berry. It is possible here to see the centuries-old stitches of plantation and removal, Bellaghy the tip of a triangle whose other points are Maghera and Moneymore. Within this territory is the history of the north as it was before Belfast became the provincial capital of a late empire, drawing in generations of country people to work in its factories. There are imprints of that empire's colonial phase everywhere in the landscape. Magherafelt, the one major town in the triangle, has a school founded on an endowment from the London guild of salters. The Moyola, which flows down from the Sperrins past Tobermore and Castledawson, and which became for Heaney a river of the mind, meanders through a tapestry of settlement and dispossession.

These were the people and places that gathered in Heaney's mind as he raced from Greece to Ireland to Sweden in a flurry of press and congratulations. He soon longed for the relative peace he had known before the Nobel announcement. Heaney had lived a hectic life of readings, writing, and social and academic engagements for decades, but the call of Sweden brought scrutiny of an entirely different order. He associated the world before with his last moments in the grounds of Epidaurus, the ancient theatre that he recognized also as a place of healing, in anticipation of new beginning. Time spent there was preparation for 'epiphany',[3] a rebirth that had its echoes in his own memories of the family doctor's visits to the farmhouse to deliver his siblings. As Heaney pictured it in 'Out of the Bag', Dr. Kerlin was of another world than ancient Greece, his eyes 'beyond-the-north-wind blue'.[4] But he was a bridge, like Asclepius, between this world and another, the poet an observer of the process of arrival. The poem is drowsy with Greece's daytime heat, and has something of Heaney's feeling for the vision of Piers Plowman in its drifting in and out of clear consciousness. The unreality of the weeks that followed Heaney's award of the Nobel is there in the poem like the

---

[3] 'Out of the Bag', *EL*.   [4] Ibid.

'heat and fumes'[5] of his childhood memory of serving as an incense bearer on pilgrimage to Lourdes. The discordance of these memories in place and time 'blinded' Heaney as he lay in 'windless light'.[6] Earlier he had compared Dr. Kerlin's bag to an 'ark'.[7] Becalmed, Heaney thinks again of his place in time.

> It was midday, mid-May, pre-tourist sunlight
> In the precincts of the god,
> The very site of the temple of Asclepius.
> I wanted nothing more than to lie down
> Under hogweed, under seeded grass
> And to be visited in the very eye of the day
> By Hygeia, his daughter, her name still clarifying
> The haven of light she was, the undarkening door.[8]

The association of light with a clearance runs deep in Heaney's poetry. It is the substance of his memory of family affection and an aspect of far sight. Light represents extension in the poems, dark stillness and pause. The panorama between is life, which registers as rain or cloudy weather, those in-between states in which the everyday happens. Heaney was most attentive to those moments when that weather broke, that conditioned surprise that he understood to be the substance of poetry. Hygeia is a figure of myth, and a figure of speech, the word 'haven' summoning Heaney's other poems of journey and refuge, the poetry a reading of the cultural barometer,

> The word deepening, clearing, like the sky
> Elsewhere on Minches, Cromarty, The Faroes.[9]

Place is an overlapping texture of sensations the poet is alive to, on the radio, in a book, by touch and sight. At the beginning of his writing life Heaney imagined this progress as a door into the dark. Now, in

---

[5] Ibid.   [6] Ibid.   [7] Ibid.   [8] Ibid.   [9] 'Glanmore Sonnets', *FW*.

Epidaurus, he sees in the goddess the light of change, the form of which is still unseen. Hygeia was a figure of cleanliness, from which the word hygiene derives. The association is entry to the underworld of Heaney's poetry, going back to 'The Strand at Lough Beg' and the ritual washing of the murdered Colum McCartney in fallen rain. Lough Beg lies in the low country north of Lough Neagh, from where you can see the new road bridge that bypasses Toome in the distance, a blue arch in the greens and browns of the water meadows. I have tried for years to walk out to its shores from the road beyond Bellaghy, but have never made it yet thanks to the cattle in the field that gives access via Church Island. Now there is a guided path out to the next promontory, threaded through sedge and ditches, and a herd of Belted Galloways, a Scottish breed of cow fit for the muddy ground. The last woods before the path ends are sanctuary to the red squirrel and a hide to watch migrating swans and geese in the shallows of the Bann as it wanders out of Lough Neagh. It is a place of slow time still, as Heaney found it, a place for

> Big-voiced scullions, herders, feelers round
> Haycocks and hindquarters, talkers in byres,
> Slow arbitrators of the burial ground.[10]

The question of judgment long occupied Heaney. Alone for a few moments in Epidaurus he wished for a new beginning, through the undarkening door. The past had more than enough ghosts, the present as many cares. The path to the future was foreshortened by time, as Heaney was becoming aware. He had thought about this moment of transition before in 'The Main of Light', the essay he wrote about art and revelation, that time when 'sweetness flows into...poetry...as a stream of light'.[11] For Heaney, this happened in poems that work as portals to another form of consciousness, such as Shakespeare created in his Sonnet Sixty:

---

[10] 'The Strand at Lough Beg', *FW*.   [11] 'The Main of Light', *FK*.

6 LATE HEANEY

> Like as the waves make towards the pebbl'd shore,
> So do our minutes hasten to their end;
> Each changing place with that which goes before,
> In sequent toil all forwards do contend.
> Nativity, once in the main of light,
> Crawls to maturity, wherewith being crown'd,
> Crooked eclipses 'gainst his glory fight,
> And Time that gave doth now his gift confound.

Shakespeare's sea of light is of a kind with Heaney's water lands, to which all the major dramas of his middle poetry have a connection.[12] But if the two poets share a point of origin, they depart in different directions. For Shakespeare, illumination is the bright stretch between childhood and later middle age. For Heaney it is a continuous possibility, a gleam or flash that is a signature of many of the poems, as if he worked for a long time at tempering vision to reality as he found it. He saw it first in the natural world, in the shimmering phosphorescence of eels, the glitter of fish scales. Later he saw it in the sky, as aurora and meteor. Later again it became the substance of all existence, a base coat that broke through the dark matter of the everyday, like the silver foil found on 'Route 110'. Heaney found a form of this poetic apparition in his reading of his Nobel predecessor, William Butler Yeats, whose 'Cold Heaven' Heaney called a 'visionary exclamation'.[13] Set in the winter of life, Yeats's poem imagines the last panorama of life as a wild horizon:

> So wild that every casual thought of that and this
> Vanished, and left but memories, that should be out of season
> With the hot blood of youth, of love crossed long ago;
> And I took all the blame out of all sense and reason,
> Until I cried and trembled and rocked to and fro,
> Riddled with light.

---

[12] For more on this about Heaney, and Irish literature more generally, read my *Ireland, Literature and the Coast: Seatangled* (Oxford University Press, 2020).

[13] 'Joy or Night: Last Things in the Poetry of W. B. Yeats and Philip Larkin', *FK*.

William Butler Yeats had arrived in Sweden in the immediate aftermath of civil war, unsure of himself before the world's cameras, which greeted him as he stepped from the train into central station. In the film footage that remains, Yeats's fur-lined coat weighs heavily on him as he looks myopically to the awaiting pressmen, no matter that he had anticipated the award for years. Heaney arrived similarly insecure of his circumstances, with the Troubles still ongoing. It is curious to think the two writers had much the same time left before them when Yeats now seems the older man. What both shared as they aged was a sense of the world underlit by presences whose apparition was substance of the world's motion. In Yeats that light darkened in his last years. In Heaney it grew and multiplied, riddled through the work like a word game in which the desire for enlightenment gave way to an acknowledgment of the unknown. The ark of Dr. Kerlin's medical bag carried mysteries as deep as the healing sanctuary of Epidaurus, an equation soon overwhelmed by the clamour and news of the Nobel.

December in Stockholm was dry and cold in the short days of winter, the locals dressed in grey and black in tune with the prevailing weather. The city is built on an archipelago of islands joined by bridges and ferries, the summer lingering in the shut-up waterside restaurants in hibernation for the new season. The buildings are low slung, which allows the short sun to linger before it dips behind the skyline of the old town, over the foreshore of which looms the bulk of the royal palace. The Heaneys stayed two islands across in the Grand Hotel. Built in the nineteenth century, it looks out onto a narrow harbour filled with tied-up tourist boats, the white hulls adding colour to the dark water, scattered with birds migrating from the further north. The scene was not too unfamiliar to Heaney, especially around the parliament, where anglers fish for salmon and sea trout, much as they do in Galway.

Everything else was new. The award of the Nobel is more than the moment of exchange between the writer and the King of Sweden. By the time Heaney made it to Stockholm he had lived under a deluge of media and social requests, congratulations, nods, and notes that came in from around the world.[14] Walking down the street became a kind of

---

[14] Heaney soon wrote to Tom Sleigh of 'the confusion and cram of mail and obligation, pageantry and business that the prize has brought in its wake', 5 January 1996, *LSH*.

performance, never mind dressing in black tie for a dinner in the city hall with hundreds of the great and good. It is hard not to imagine the whole experience as passing through a kind of portal, not unlike the change that happens in 'The Tollund Man in Springtime', the poet reawakened 'to revel in the spirit'.[15] Certainly Heaney and his family were aware of the cost of the Nobel as well as its benefits, in particular the stripping away of one further layer of privacy they had already struggled to protect. Still, visiting Stockholm today and walking down the steps of the Nobel Museum into the cobbled square of the old town is to follow Heaney's own steps into another life, the beginning of which was marked by taking his place by the physicists, doctors, and peace makers who sat beside him on the stage, each wondering at their circumstances.

Heaney's acceptance speech was a gathering of the lines that had led him to this moment. There was surprise in the idea that he had travelled so far beyond anything he might have imagined as a child, and recognition too in the long familiarity Heaney had with the writings of William Butler Yeats, who too had stood here decades earlier, shaken by violence but optimistic of some respite, hope a nest built in the ruins of the past. For Heaney that past stretched back through his earliest memories in rural Derry to the older stories of another natural healing in St Kevin and the Blackbird, and beyond that to images without words, the *bas-relief* he studied in the museum at Sparta before the news of the Nobel Prize broke. That stonework spoke to him as evidence of the durability of art, and of its rootedness. It pictured a bird and beast held by the music of Orpheus, which Heaney recognized as an ancient version of his own practice, of the 'self-enrapturing man'.[16]

When it was time for Heaney to speak, he began with familiar self-deprecation. Heaney's journey to this moment in Stockholm was a long one, and unlikely. His first steps traced familiar ground well-patterned by the generations before, the circumference of their collective experience the townlands bordered by the Moyola and Lough Neagh. The outside world was heard, not felt, its registers the radio and the rumble

---

[15] 'The Tollund Man in Springtime', *DC*.   [16] *NL*.

of the goods train, two sonic signatures that register frequently in Heaney's poetry. As Heaney talked he invited the idea that his work had been to give voice to the community that nurtured him, the 'utter silence'[17] perforated by a poetry that began to speak in the voices it hears around it. This was a surprisingly worldly chorus, at least through the transmissions of the BBC, which looped into the Mossbawn farmhouse through a wire strung to a nearby tree. If the life of the earth had not changed for centuries, the air was 'alive and signalling',[18] the young poet awake to the frequencies of elsewhere, which at this time in the early forties was troubled with war and destruction. The idea of reception begins a theme that builds throughout Heaney's acceptance speech, which is his consideration of William Butler Yeats as his predecessor. Heaney was the fourth Irish writer to win the Nobel Prize for Literature, but Shaw and Beckett barely register in his Stockholm address.[19] Yeats, however, was a writer whose art was a form of reception, his poetry and prose the channelling of frequencies whose contours once drawn revealed the shape of the world, as it was and could be. Heaney did not share Yeats's reactionary interest in the ordering power of such insight. Absorbing the news of world war, Heaney never experienced 'terror',[20] becoming instead 'deliberate'[21] in his listening as he grew older. The word is typical of Heaney's punning style, hinting as it does of deliberation, of hesitation as much as of intention. Different, however, is Heaney's tone, which for once is without self-rebuke.

One of the signature transitions that this speech, and this award, represented for Heaney was a movement beyond the enclosures that marked the mental geography of his poetry before. These were of the north, of politics and the one side over another. These pressures did not go away after the prize. Indeed they were felt brutally during it. But they had a different place in his mind, and his life, afterwards, which signalled a shift generally in the way that he wrote. Just as the passing train had caused the water in a bucket to ripple in widening circles so did

---

[17] Ibid.   [18] Ibid.
[19] The previous recipients were Samuel Beckett (1969), George Bernard Shaw (1925), and William Butler Yeats (1923).
[20] *NL.*   [21] Ibid.

Heaney's turns of the radio dial open his ear to Dublin, Leipzig, Oslo, Stuttgart, Stockholm, and Warsaw, Heaney's friendship with the Polish Nobel laureate Milosz another ghost in the machine. The speech is in this way an assembly of premonitions, the foundations for which are decades of reading, writing, talking, and thinking. It is also, by necessity, a departure. Heaney imagined his journey to this moment as a walk over stepping stones across the river of life. In Stockholm, before the assembly, that metaphor no longer seemed to hold, the gravity of the moment inducing a weightlessness that turned stone to air, inviting a 'space-walk'.[22] The idea connected to a poem he had written, and which would be included as 'The Gravel Walks' in *The Spirit Level*. The line that joined Stockholm to Heaney's attic in Dublin's Sandymount was the invitation 'to walk on air against your better judgment',[23] a turn against the rooted cautions of the north. 'The Gravel Walks' is its own kind of space-walk, drawing a memory of sun and the riverbank that was to become Heaney's abiding late motif. It rises now in the borderland between land and water, gravel the broken medium of both, 'Beautiful in or out of the river'.[24] The poem has a cast of familiar landsmen drawn to the river for its bounty, a crew gathered later again in 'The Eelworks'.

The sluice of these watery images over the stony graft of farm-labour is of a kind with Heaney's revision of his calling in Stockholm. Poetry now is the inclusion of all things in a brighter light than before, shadows and ghosts the relics of a past that has lessening purchase, Heaney's art recognized for its 'truth to life, in every sense of that phrase'.[25] How he might do this is part of what follows in his speech, which is as close as Heaney came to a manifesto. His company in this enterprise are the poets he cites as influences: Keats, Chaucer, Lowell, and Bishop. It is in its way a healing list, written in the traditions of an English and an American literature that is outside the canon of twentieth-century Irish poetry. It is a premonition too, especially in Heaney's citation of Keats's poem 'To Autumn', whose closing lines invite the dreamscape that Heaney returns to near the end of his life in his Virgilian Derry, the

---

[22] Ibid.   [23] Ibid.   [24] 'The Gravel Walks', *SL*.   [25] *NL*.

insects on the river, the 'gathering swallows' in the air, in preparation for the long journey ahead.

Heaney's late poetry is a panorama of the senses, the portal to which opens in this Stockholm speech, the poet taken out of the here and now and transported for that brief, unlikely moment to that assembly in Stockholm where the impossible is real. The realization invited Heaney to create a different declension of poets whose work extended beyond the known and familiar to the strange and visionary. Stevens, Rilke, Dickinson, and Eliot offer a different way to think of the relationship between poetry and a world whose foundations are built in violence and exclusion. The consequences of this for the artist are not abstract, as Heaney was aware. Escaping with his young family to Wicklow in the early seventies he had felt exiled and diminished, the brutalities of the earlier twentieth century a parallel to his own Irish troubles. Thinking of the Russian writer Osip Mandelstam, Heaney returned in Stockholm to one of his most powerful poems of that earlier period, 'Exposure'.[26] The winter woods of that poem have spoken to me for years of the cold isolation of the Troubles, that damp seepage of the centuries that worked its way into every hope of betterment. Then Heaney had no answer but to wait and watch:

> I am neither internee nor informer;
> An inner émigré, a grown long-haired
> And thoughtful; a wood-kerne
> Escaped from the massacre,
> Taking protective colouring
> From bole and bark, feeling
> Every wind that blows;
> Who, blowing up these sparks
> For their meagre heat, have missed
> The once in a lifetime portent,
> The comet's pulsing rose.[27]

---

[26] Osip Mandelstam (1891–1938) was born in Warsaw and died after arrest, torture, exile, and imprisonment in Soviet work camps. Heaney wrote about Osip and Nadezhda Mandelstam in the *London Review of Books* on 20 August 1981 after reading Nadezhda's memoir, *Hope against Hope*.
[27] 'Exposure', N.

The lesson is a complex one, hedged between self-doubt and the absolute conviction that the indignities of history, which were not, in the north as in so many other 'wounded'[28] places Heaney mentions, in the past, could be overcome, not by equal force but by individual imagination. This seems a scant answer to the Troubles and all the rest, a litany of which Heaney cites throughout his speech. But where there was once melancholy that the revolutionary moment might have passed by, too late, there emerges understanding that the operations of the human mind in the practice of art create a space for joy in excess of terror. The idea unbalances the Yeatsian formula that social balance required equity between reality and justice. Heaney makes poetry the holy ghost in a creed that opened the door for new language, and new feeling, in the work to come. His cue was in Anna Akhmatova, whose discovery of the power of art in the horror of Stalinist Russia resonated with Heaney, even in his more 'protected'[29] circumstances. The lines of Akhmatova that were in Heaney's mind as he spoke were from 'Requiem':

> During the frightening years of the Yezhov terror, I
> spent seventeen months waiting in prison queues in
> Leningrad. One day, somehow, someone 'picked me out'.
> On that occasion there was a woman standing behind me,
> her lips blue with cold, who, of course, had never in
> her life heard my name. Jolted out of the torpor
> characteristic of all of us, she said into my ear
> (everyone whispered there)—'Could one ever describe
> this?' And I answered—'I can.' It was then that
> something like a smile slid across what had previously
> been just a face.[30]

Two images extend from Akhmatova's poem into the progress of Heaney's address. The first is the idea of being picked out, which Heaney

---

[28] *NL*.   [29] Ibid.
[30] Anna Akhmatova (1889–1966) was a Russian poet, scholar, and translator. Her books were banned in Russia from 1925 to 1940. Heaney visited the Fountain House in Moscow, where she had once lived, in the early summer of 2003. To Dennis O'Driscoll, 27 June 2003, *LSH*.

relates to the story of a Catholic workman who survived the murder of his Protestant colleagues by being pulled, unwittingly, out of a firing line.[31] The second is immediate, and longer-lasting in context of the poetry. This is Heaney's admission of joy into the work, a relief, literal and figurative, that diminished the shadows of the previous decades in the clear light of day. He described this change as a straightening-up, a lifting of the weight that he had assumed he must carry, the desire 'to make space in my reckoning and imagining for the marvellous as well as for the murderous'.[32]

For Heaney the thread between the human and the celestial is a line drawn by an art of cosmic dimension, grounded in the hands that hold its ends. This is the orientation of later poems like 'A Kite for Aibhinn' and the outline of wider dimension in his writing, the panorama of which works eventually into the elevation of his late summer Derry skies. It is a land-, water-, and skyscape that contains the historical and the contemporary, the terrible and the transformative, as it does in a poem like 'Polish Sleepers'. The effect is to imagine place as a theatre in which the most intimate of private feelings can survive beside the most public events, however cruel. The Nobel speech is a summary of Heaney's arrival at this awareness, and a gesture forward. Two of its mentors are Wordsworth and Yeats, the earlier poets' explorations of the human condition in times of turbulence significant for Heaney as exemplary attempts to shape the moment to poetry. For poetry, not history, and not in the end even place, is Heaney's subject. This poetry is a practice as much as a form, an awareness as much as an aesthetic. Its tutors are Mandelstam and Akhmatova, its symbolic figures legend and myth, like St Kevin, whose kindness to the nesting blackbird signals a patience and a dexterity that Heaney much valued. It is a work of translation between the local and the global, an attitude that Heaney saw in the small things.

---

[31] The Kingsmill massacre took place on 5 January 1976 in Co. Armagh. Ten Protestant workmen were murdered, and one survived his wounds. The single Catholic present was let go.
[32] *NL.*

In Stockholm he remembered the last day of his old life before the Nobel, wandering anonymous in a small museum in Sparta. There he was captivated by an antique votive statue, an offering to Orpheus by some unknown poet that Heaney sketched and noted. The durability and sincerity of the thing impressed him. It reminded Heaney too that he was one voice in a millennia old chorus, which for once he could orchestrate as he liked, the moment of the Nobel a singular opportunity to shape his company. The issue was to some degree delicate given the small confines of an Irish literary scene that had its own jealousies. Heaney sidestepped the problem by avoiding to name any of his contemporaries and turning again to the Yeats of late middle age, of 'Meditations in Time of Civil War' and 'The Municipal Gallery Revisited'. The lessons of each were of perseverance in the face of violent upheaval, and of the building of artistic community. Both were foundations of Heaney's progress to this point, but neither alone could frame the new freedoms Heaney hoped for his art after Stockholm. It was less that the Nobel changed anything for Heaney as a writer, however the weight of expectation, as a public figure as much as a writer, was upon him. Instead, the space-walk to reduced gravity was still troubled by events in the north and conditioned pessimism in the self. The Nobel speech is a charter in reply, a charge to 'grow up to that which we stored up as we grew'.[33] It is a miniature of the longer and more measured account of the self that he gathered in the interviews with Denis O'Driscoll in *Stepping Stones*.[34] The occasion of the Nobel Speech was Heaney's most public moment. With Homer on his mind he used it to declare the beginning of his new journey.

> Poetic form is both the ship and the anchor. It is at once a buoyancy and a steadying, allowing for the simultaneous gratification of whatever is centrifugal and whatever is centripetal in mind and body. And

---

[33] Ibid.
[34] Heaney worried about this too, up until the last minute, in 'a panic for weeks' just before the book's publication in case he had erred in choosing a book of interviews as the format for what was, in effect, an autobiography. Partly thanks to his friendship with O'Driscoll, he gathered himself and published the book. To Paul Keegan and Stephen Page, 15 February 2008, *LSH*.

it is by such means that Yeats's work does what the necessary poetry always does, which is to touch the base of our sympathetic nature while taking in at the same time the unsympathetic nature of the world to which that nature is constantly exposed.[35]

Heaney's rivering prose mimics the twists and turns of his mind over the previous decades, his measure of time and experience a constant weight on his sense of self and becoming. In the early phases of his poetry this led to self-questioning, and often rebuke. In the later it leads to a self-reflexive twisting that can become repetitive. Between these habits there emerges a space for empathy, which is why Heaney had 'Exposure' in his head as he wrote his address. That poem stood out for decades as the representation of a landscape perfectly realized to incorporate the personal with the contemporary and the historical. It ended with a forlorn hope for some visionary escape from these circumstances, a hope the later Heaney revises into the illumination of the landscape itself. The key is Heaney's image of himself as a 'wood-kerne',[36] a description that has associations with defeat, dispossession, and rebellion. Hidden in this is the human integration with the trees, an image Heaney takes up in his idea to take refuge in every bole and bark. What was once a retreat becomes in the later poems an infusion that is basis for an empathy that extends beyond the human, into the animals, trees, plants, earth, water, and sky. The field work for this new being is in the hands-on empathy of a poem like 'Human Chain', which Heaney took as emblem for what was to be his last collection. Its application into the late land-, river-, and skyscapes of the poems that follow Stockholm create a luminous sense of place that is animated by a consideration for being that makes Heaney's Derry a poetic imaginary the equivalent of Wordsworth's Lake District.[37] The portals of this imaginary commons are still visible in the townlands around Bellaghy, and part of the point of this book is to connect the later poems to the places Heaney had in

---

[35] *NL*.   [36] 'Exposure', *N*.
[37] The comparison might even be extended to Heaney's move to Glanmore, which had its connections with the Synge family. To Heaney, that 'was a richness, but it didn't have any effect on what I was doing. Grasmere, with the Wordsworths' cottage, probably meant more to me at the time'. *SS*, 208.

mind. Together they mark the outlines of Heaney's confirmed late philosophy, which was that, past regret and shame and fear, 'our very solitudes and distresses are creditable, in so far as they, too, are an earnest of our veritable human being'.[38]

These closing words of Heaney's acceptance speech opened a new world of engagements and encumbrances for the poet. On top of the regular round of readings and addresses he had committed to before the Nobel, new waves of interviews and appearances rose before him, never mind the flood of congratulations. The whole made him feel that he was a travel agent more than an artist, much as his poetry had long been on the move, in tractors, buses, cars, and airplanes. I taught later at the University of North Carolina at Chapel Hill, which has a long and distinguished history of the study and teaching of Irish literature. One of my first surprises there was to see photographs of Heaney at a pig-picking, which was the slow barbeque of a whole hog at the home of one of the faculty members, himself a distinguished Joycean. Heaney was beaming, perhaps because someone had produced a bottle of moonshine. He was there because some enterprising professors had arranged for his invitation to give the commencement address the Spring after Heaney was awarded the Nobel.

Heaney spoke in Chapel Hill on the 12th of May, a date he recognized as the traditional time of the hiring fair in rural Ulster. Those connections were much in his mind, with the links between this part of the American South and the north of Ireland so present in shared names and history (and Heaney remembered as he spoke of one of the university's first professors, a Reverend David Ker, late of Trinity College Dublin). Heaney was not a natural commencement speaker, disinclined as he was by nature to give advice on how anyone else should live their life. But the moment called for direction and his was simple, if difficult to practice, and proceeding from his attachment in Stockholm months previously to self-verification. To Heaney, inner-truth was essential life, and verification its watchword, the danger otherwise of 'settling into whatever profile the world prepares for you'.[39] There was less poetry in

[38] *NL*.   [39] Commencement Address, UNC Chapel Hill, 12 May 1996.

the Carolina speech, but what was there was fundamental, Milton and Wordsworth the two writers who spoke through Heaney to this generation of younger people at a way-marker in their own journeys, *Paradise Lost* and *The Prelude* language and reflection enough for any life.[40]

Their apparition reminds again how Heaney was, like Shaw and Beckett, an Irish Nobel Laureate whose literary version of Ireland was representative of the island's tangled global histories more than it was confirmation of some apparent, inherent tendency to poetry, drama, or prose. Heaney's return to Wordsworth signals his investment in the locality as the wellspring of aesthetic reflection, the given and the intimate the portals to some wider truths, and not their impediment. Perhaps this had always been the case, as might be read in his thran reactions to being marginalized as a kind of new Kavanagh of the Troubles in the early seventies. The difference now was Heaney's understanding of that locality as a radiant possible place, significant of the deepest marks of time and presence. No longer was the poet downcast among the dying leaves in search of falling fragments of enlightenment. Instead there is a steadying, a centring, and a more even distribution of insight as the verification of poetic practice. It is there in the rhythms of the later poems, and in their subjects, the steady collective work of a poem like 'Human Chain' a statement of art's form and necessity.

In Stockholm, the recent memory of Greece had taken Heaney back into the violent history of the twentieth century, and forward to some hope of reconciliation. The present was more uncertain, the rush of the two months since Pylos a surge of public activity in which there was little time to think or reflect, never mind to write. The Nobel is a waypoint whoever wins it, and however they may try to avoid it (and Samuel Beckett was horrified when he learned that he had won it on holiday in Tunisia, agreeing to an interview with Swedish television on condition no questions were asked). The prize has a gravity that affects the balance a writer has with readers, friends, editors, and critics, a balance that is

---

[40] Of the two, John Milton (1608–1674) has the more complex relationship with the history of Ireland, Milton having served in Cromwell's administration. That history is less there in Heaney's response to Milton's writing; indeed Heaney took part in a reading of the entirety of *Paradise Lost* at Trinity College Dublin in 2012.

often hard-won and uneasily kept. By 1995 Heaney was one of Ireland's most famous living writers and had been for two decades and more, lodged in Oxford and Harvard, published by Faber, and by nature connected to circles of friends and admirers that ringed the world.[41] He had had long opportunity to think about how to measure the weight of this social obligation against the lift of the imagination in his poetry, often looking to the night sky for celestial objects that moved with mass and light, moon and meteorite. He returned to the idea in the closing lines of his Stockholm speech, poetry a ship and anchor, 'a buoyancy and a steadying'.[42]

It took Heaney another six years to find the form to join the weightless and the irresistible in his 'Sonnets from Hellas'. The six poems that make up this sequence range over Heaney's experiences in Greece, in Ireland, and in the United States, where all converged in Arcadia. The richness of the agricultural landscape and the darkness of the ancient myths had their corollaries in Heaney's experience, which still shuddered before sectarian murder at home in the north. Peace had its province on the west coast, as it did in Ireland too, the third sonnet with a view of

> *Barbounia* schooled below the balcony—
> Shadows on shelving sand in sandy Pylos.[43]

The inland sea of Lough Neagh was never far from Heaney's imagination, and with it the River Moyola and the farmyard pump, helmeted like an ancient Greek and dripping water.[44] After Stockholm, Heaney put shape on the Nobel by returning poetically to Pylos as a new beginning shaped by wave and tide.

---

[41] The publication of the letters is invaluable to the witness of Heaney's ascent, from the publication of *Death of a Naturalist* in 1965 to his receipt of the Nobel thirty years later. Of particular interest is his friendship with Charles Monteith, the Lisburn-born editor at Faber who was the first to contact him from the press after reading some of Heaney's poems in the *New Statesman* in late 1964. See Heaney's reply to Charles Monteith, 2 February 1965, *LSH*.
[42] *NL*. [43] 'Sonnets from Hellas', *EL*.
[44] That pump was, to Heaney, the centre of his first awareness: 'I would begin with the Greek word *omphalos*, meaning the navel, and hence the stone that marked the centre of the world, and repeat it...until its blunt and falling music becomes the music of somebody pumping water at the pump outside our back door. It is County Derry in the early 1940s', 'Mossbawn', *FK*.

I woke to the world there like Telemachos,
Young again in the whitewashed light of morning
That flashed on the ceiling like an early warning
From myself to be more myself in the mast-bending
Marine breeze, to key the understanding
To that image of the bow strung as a lyre...[45]

There are many threads here, the sonnet sequence a labyrinth through which the reader is led from dark to light. That journey is not without its losses, the classicist Robert Fitzgerald a shade beside the murdered Sean Brown, ambushed in Heaney's home place.[46] In return its consolations are of the mind and body, the poetry a musculature of sensation, embodied, enriched, and persevering. This is an art of underground channels that feed ideas far from their source, like the pipes that water the walnut farm Heaney passed in the Greek mountains, a technique 'Known in Hellas, probably, since Hesiod'.[47] It grows from a poet newly prepared to show himself in a landscape changed irrevocably by time and experience. The advice to free himself had been administered before, as it had from the shade of Joyce in 'Station Island'.[48] But like the ghost it faded. Now the poet was irredeemably a public man, even if the question remained of how to live the role. 'Sonnets from Hellas' has the beginning of an answer, Heaney in wild career through the roads before Mount Parnassus, his head light,

...hyper, boozed, borean
As we bowled back down towards the olive plain
Siren-tyred and manic on the horn
Round hairpin bends looped like boustrophedon.[49]

---

[45] 'Sonnets from Hellas', *EL*.
[46] Fitzgerald was a translator and classical scholar. Heaney met Fitzgerald during his time at Harvard, as we shall read again later when we come to the intellectual and social circle he found there, especially with regard to Heaney's admiration for Czeslaw Milosz.
[47] 'Sonnets from Hellas', *EL*.
[48] 'Station Island' is the title sequence of Heaney's 1984 collection of the same name. The poem is composed of twelve sections that imitate a pilgrimage to St Patrick's Purgatory at Lough Derg, Co. Donegal. A series of figures appear to the speaker in visions that offer perspective on the poet's own predicament as a writer and a witness. The poem is one of Heaney's first sustained attempts to think of death as a condition of light and weather.
[49] 'Sonnets from Hellas', *EL*.

The zigzag lines of an ancient poem written from left to right, and right to left and back again suggest something of the manic years that led from Pylos to Stockholm and after. For my own part I remember a calmer figure, a quiet man who would turn up to poetry readings in Dublin and sit in the back row, looking for no attention beyond solidarity with younger writers.

That city was new to me then, having arrived at Trinity College Dublin after Belfast. Heaney stayed with me, through Belfast, Dublin, and beyond, and I have written about him often, and thought about him more. I came to appreciate the later poems in a roundabout way, in large part through the interest Heaney had in islands, in coasts, and in rivers, which surfaces so beautifully in his versions of Virgil. This brought me back in turn to rural Derry, to the Moyola in summer, the ditches long ribbons of whitethorn and bird in the June time. These are the landscapes of late Heaney, which the poet returned to and remade in face of age and illness, the late poems panoramas of water and light that give the work new depth and dimension.

Late Heaney. Nicholas Allen, Oxford University Press. © Nicholas Allen 2026.
DOI: 10.1093/9780198985419.003.0001

2
Landscapes

The landscapes of Seamus Heaney's later poetry are territories of the earth, air, and water. They are configurations of space and time through which presences pass in different weathers, environments the poems draw from the materials of memory and experience. The origin point of all is the boggy delta of Lough Neagh by the mouth of the River Bann, an inland estuary that shaped the uncertain ground of Heaney's poetry. Heaney mapped this place early on. His first major experiment in writing poetry in a chain of place-based associations was 'A Lough Neagh Sequence', which was published in the *University Review* in the winter of 1967 and collected subsequently in *Door into the Dark*. Its seven poems chart the intersections between the life cycle of the eels that spawn in the Lough, the fishermen who catch them, and the imagery that Heaney sought to represent them. This last was a question of time and place as much as of language as Heaney experimented with patterns and images that give the work an air of premonition that makes the soon-to-follow Troubles poems so haunting, because so foretold.

In 'A Lough Neagh Sequence', the weight of history had not quite assumed its deadly gravity. Neither was Heaney's head then quite in the present, tinkering as he was with making poems in the circular patterns of Celtic art. Water is the interlace of this first work, as it was to remain. Its dominion was the north of pre-Christianity, its demands of sacrifice and ritual, which had devolved in the modern world into the seasonal repetition of harvest and chore. Seeing this, Heaney works his poems like cast lines. In doing so, he anticipated a language that stayed with him to the very end, a late poem like 'The Eelworks' already summoned in the sketchy outline of the Lough. The drift of 'Casualty' is there too, as are the forms of self-questioning that the middle Heaney carried as a moral burden. Images of the horizon are also there, especially in the curved arc as Heaney imagined it, softened at the last by the evening sun. His Lough sky is raucous and gull-filled, Heaney looking up, however we tend to think of him as a writer with the head down, gone to earth.

'A Lough Neagh Sequence' is in the first instance about the people Heaney knew around the water's edges. It is dedicated to the fishermen who spent a small part of their year harvesting the eels from the Lough. The occupation fascinated him, half in and half out of the water. The eel fishers themselves refused to learn how to swim, which informs the idea in 'Up the Shore' that the lough 'will claim a victim every year'.[1] The grim fatedness of this fits with Heaney's subsequent correlation of the northern with tribalism and sacrifice. In context of his surfacing as a major Irish writer, the link between drowning and resignation ties Heaney back to his interest in Synge's stories of the fishermen of the Aran islands.[2] The young Heaney shifts that western panorama of the literary revival eastward, back to the contested territories off the north's shore. In this telling, the Lough is 'the scar left by the Isle of Man',[3] as if the one was made by the leaving of the other. An environmental awareness is there too in the clipped observation of changes in the waterscape caused by human interference, the eels caught in gates and tanks by the Lough mouth as they leave for the outer sea. This mixes with the folky rhythms of the fishermen themselves, who work the water with 'a sense of fair play in the game',[4] custodians of the catch, and the balance it requires. These quick sketches give way to 'Beyond Sargasso', the second poem in the sequence. Its twenty-six lines turn on the word 'Against', which gives the poem a tidal pull, out and back into the Lough. The Sargasso is where immature eels congregate,

> half-way
> across the Atlantic,
> sure as the satellite's
> insinuating pull
> in the ocean, as true
> to his orbit.[5]

---

[1] 'A Lough Neagh Sequence', *DD*.
[2] Indeed, 'Synge on Aran' is one of Heaney's first published poems in *Death of a Naturalist*.
[3] 'A Lough Neagh Sequence', *DD*.   [4] Ibid.   [5] Ibid.

The correspondence between depth and height is of the substance of the later poems, when the thin line of earth becomes a horizon between the under- and the overworld. The idea has not taken mortal shape in 'A Lough Neagh Sequence', at least in human terms. Embodiment is there in form of the late sixties space race, the silver gleam of satellites and moonmen the analogue to eel skin and fish scale. The second half of the poem devolves into word pictures of the eel as abstract being, Heaney searching for a clipped vocabulary that forms the eel as muscle and intent, and not a symbol. This is where the later, mythic energy of the seventies poems comes from, Heaney summoning the invisible by drawing it in relation to definite terms, among 'ebb, current, rock'.[6]

There is a flirtation with a more violent language too, 'abort' and 'hungering'[7] two ripples on the surface picture, which is striking since the third poem in the sequence, 'Bait', bears such an uncanny relation to Heaney's later 'Casualty'. 'Casualty' is a eulogy for Louis O'Neill, a fisherman and older companion who died in a bomb explosion after Bloody Sunday. 'Bait' precedes these future terrors but has already the vocabulary to confront them. In 'Bait',

> Lamps dawdle in the field at midnight.
> The fishermen meanwhile,
> draw steady and he'll come.[8]

In 'Casualty', mourners move

> With the habitual
> Slow consolation
> Of a dawdling engine,
> The line lifted, hand
> Over fist, cold sunshine
> On the water[9]

---

[6] Ibid.   [7] Ibid.   [8] Ibid.   [9] 'Casualty', FW.

Both poems work at the relationship between surface and actuality, fretting at the depths that poetry enters blind. The mechanism is all, whether line, shovel, hook, or pen, each an object that takes meaning from its actions. In the earlier Heaney this gives the poetry a gravity that is material. In the later, it achieves a lift that is beyond the poet in his beginnings. The medium for this transition is Heaney's openness to illumination, which extends from the handheld lamps of the fishermen in 'Bait' to the aurora skies of 'North', and after that again to 'Electric Light' and that great dome of the sky by 'The Riverbank Field'. For now, Heaney looks back to the clay, the worm tunnels a miniature in waiting of the manmade underground he would enter decades later in London. Read like this, it could be said that the architecture of Heaney's poetry was there in large part from near the beginning. Over time, his sense of scale, time, and illumination changed. But the words that bound the whole together remained. These keystones give the whole work its bearing, both in its direction and its weight-bearing load.

The Heaney who wrote 'A Lough Neagh Sequence' might have wavered if he knew of the struggles he would shortly face. The letters of the early to mid-seventies share his worries about the situation in the north, and about providing for his family having moved south from Belfast to Wicklow and then Dublin.[10] In mitigation, he focused on his craft. The fourth and fifth poems of the Lough Neagh sequence have the titles 'Setting' and 'Lifting', images of construction that are in keeping with a general idea of steady progress. 'Setting' describes the trawl of worm-hooked lines behind the fishermen's row boats in the Lough. Even here, there is a sense of Heaney's later bearing towards the horizon as birds wait for cast-off bait and side catch.

> The gulls fly and umbrella overhead,
> Treading air as soon as the line runs out,
> Responsive acolytes above the boat.[11]

---

[10] This migration is traced in personal detail in the *LSH*, which captures the stress, and sometimes the excitement, of bringing up a family and sustaining a marriage through a transitional time, with varying degrees of security beyond the one constant, which was the Heaneys' affection for each other.
[11] 'Casualty', *FW*.

That umbrella is the dome of the sky in miniature, the poem a geometry of height and breadth. The strategy will come up again later when we consider Heaney's reading of Virgil, but the idea has its early Christian corollary too, as 'acolytes' suggests. In *Seeing Things*, Heaney wrote another sequence called 'Lightenings', which plays on this dual idea of lift and enlightenment. In it, the monks at Clonmacnoise are at prayer when a ship sails in afloat on the air.[12] Its anchor catches in the oratory and one of its crew struggles to free it.

> 'This man can't bear our life here and will drown,'
> The abbot said, 'unless we help him.' So
> They did, the freed ship sailed, and the man climbed back
> Out of the marvellous as he had known it.[13]

That thread begins in 'Lifting', a 'high boat'[14] winding in the morning catch, just as Heaney's description of the eels gathered in a barrel might be from the end of his career, not the beginning. In 'Lifting', the eels are a

> furling, slippy
> Haul, a knot of back and pewter belly[15]

In 'Eelworks', from *Human Chain*, there is the

> Slither of a fellow,
> A young eel, greasy grey
> And rightly wriggle-spined,
> Not yet the blueblack
> Slick-backed waterwork
> I'd live to reckon with,
> My old familiar
> Pearl-purl
> Selkie-streaker.[16]

---

[12] Clonmacnoise is a monastic site near Athlone on the River Shannon, which was founded in the sixth century by St Ciarán. It was a place of European learning, with a still extant panorama of round towers and high crosses.
[13] 'Lightenings', *ST*.   [14] 'A Lough Neagh Sequence', *DD*.   [15] Ibid.
[16] 'Eelworks', *HC*.

All of which takes us back to 'Casualty' by that word 'purl', which Heaney used there to describe the slow turn of the screw under water. Sequence is hardly a word to describe this cross-hatched technique, which over time Heaney worked into a style. The raw materials of memory and the words that attend it are here in this earliest Lough Neagh poem. Like elvers, they travel far and out, magnetized to return at the last. The idea of this transit was in Heaney's mind as he wrote, even if he could not have been aware of its future dimensions. Instead, he sensed the cyclical nature of the journey, rounded like a hook, with open end. This is the subject of the sixth poem, 'The Return', which follows the eel on its final journey out into the ocean depths. Commas are the signature of this liquid style, such as Heaney perfected in the opening verses of 'North' a few years later. In 'The Return', there are

> new trenches, sunk pipes,
> swamps, running streams, the lough,
> the river.[17]

This water world opens the poem out into its northern dimensions, which Heaney takes further into the unknown, past Malin Head and Tory Island. He knit these zones into a poem later in 'The Shipping Forecast', which is its own reading of the weather and place as prognosis. 'A Lough Neagh Sequence' ends too with a 'Vision' by a tributary of this inner sea, a young boy watchful at night of the eels' return, 'in riverbank/Fields'.[18] Here at the beginning is the end, the panorama of life and age set on the Derry stage, a bearing Heaney never forgot, but worked into the fundamental co-ordinates of his poetry. This is the first time the riverbank appears so in his work; it does not return until *Human Chain*, in the same words, weathered by life. In the beginning, it is a flat panorama, a portal between earth and water. By the end, it is a point of perspective, a vantage from which to see the motion between this world and whatever follows. Heaney had been aware of death from a young age because of the terrible accident that killed his brother, a tragedy that haunted the first family home for his parents, and which contributed to

---

[17] 'A Lough Neagh Sequence', *DD*. [18] Ibid.

their leaving.[19] His 'Vision' of mortality is mediated through Lough Neagh by the anxiety of drowning, the eels he sees 'like hatched fears'[20] in water. The poem has as yet no capacity, or the poet no craft, to mend these psychic fractures in images of resolution. The late weather of a summer evening is not there; however, there is the awareness of light, 'Phosphorescent'.[21]

In Heaney then, landscape is the accumulation of experience in the pervious place of memory, a bog meadow of the imagination expressed in words weathered by use. In this world, the townland of Anahorish was a little island, connected to the outside world by the wireless, and part of a chain of human associations that extended to neighbours and school, and from there to Derry, Belfast, Dublin, Wicklow, and beyond. As a child, Heaney's far horizon was marked by Slemish, the flat-topped mountain that St Patrick preached from.[22] Slemish is visible for miles from the north-eastern shores of Lough Neagh, elevated on the escarpment that drops on the other side to the Glens of Antrim, the sea, and Ailsa Craig across the water. Heaney's sense of his early place as prehistorical was generated partly from its physical setting, Bellaghy in a bowl of fields and sky, its connection to the outside world its roads, its railways, its streams and rivers. As he read, travelled, and lived, he returned to these landscapes as a painter might, picturing them in different light from different angles. The drenched melancholy of the Troubles gives way to a sunny evening by the Moyola, the water meadows by Lough Neagh parched in the summer memories of farmyard and kitchen.

This sense of transition invites the question of how these landscapes bear the imprint of a lifetime of reading and experience. Heaney had a series of fascinations, with Ted Hughes, Czeslaw Milosz, with *Beowulf* and the *Aeneid*, and had a lifelong correspondence with his contemporary, the painter Barrie Cooke.[23] There are traces of all of them in the

---

[19] Christopher Heaney was killed at the age of four in a car accident in 1953. His death is commemorated in one of Heaney's best known early poems, 'Mid-Term Break'. The family moved not long after.
[20] 'A Lough Neagh Sequence', *DD*.   [21] Ibid.
[22] 'In emotional and familiar terms, I am in fact more an Antrim man than a Sperrin man', he wrote, 'Ballymena and Slemish were points of imaginative as well as physical geography to me'. To Francis Murphy, 16 December 1989, *LSH*.
[23] The Heaneys knew Barrie Cooke and his Dutch wife Sonja Landweer from the early 70s, and both figure regularly in Heaney's poetry and letters.

work, both hidden and declared. Landscape, then, is a term for seeing and absorbing, a subject for translation and revision more than the grounds for definitive statement. At least it was for Heaney, who guarded the secret sources of his writing with a determination slightly at odds with the openness associated with his public persona. He had let, in mid-career, Michael Parker visit the specific shallows of the Moyola he regarded as an imaginative well for his consciousness and was horrified when he learned that the place might become public on terms other than his own.[24] Heaney's personal hinterlands shaped the public poetry. But the process was his to manage, territorial and guarded. It resonated with William Wordsworth's sense of place in *The Prelude*, which Heaney quoted approvingly in his early essay, 'Feeling into Words'.

> The hiding places of my power
> Seem open; I approach, and then they close;
> I see by glimpses now; when age comes on,
> May scarcely see at all, and I would give,
> While yet we may, as far as words can give,
> A substance and a life to what I feel...

Heaney had a love for the sideways talk of his home place, the known fact a thing to be walked and worked around. Revelation was a slow process, a ritual, measured by a chronology different from the minute cartography of criticism. Its poetic shape is the many shades who take human form in Heaney's poetry, from the bog bodies to the Troubles dead. These shapes take more generous form as Heaney's poetry proceeds, the brutality represented in the earlier work giving way to 'Tollund Man in Springtime', 'spirited...into the street'.[25] In this, they are less signals from the past than signs of the future, those premonitions of hidden power that Wordsworth felt, clothed in the language of Heaney's own place and time.

---

[24] 'For example, the Moyola sandbed', Heaney wrote. 'That place I marked so that you could *see* it. If any photograph appeared, or map that gave access, I would be devastated'. To Michael Parker, 12 July 1988, *LSH*.
[25] 'Tollund Man in Springtime', *DC*.

Even as he became absorbed in the circuits of world literature, an old hand at lectures, readings and signings, often at the price of exhaustion, he kept his private places to himself. The first and most abiding of these was Glanmore cottage in County Wicklow, which Heaney had rented from Anne Saddlemyer when he left Belfast with his family in the early 70s.[26] This was a fraught time for Heaney and his wife, friend and first reader Marie, the perverse security of a university position in Belfast during the Troubles exchanged for the uncertainties of life as a professional writer, a career Heaney soon subvented with a return to teaching. Glanmore was a lair and a refuge, a place of dark repair. Heaney identified it as the single site where he felt confirmed as a writer, secure in his place and work, a forge as much as a dwelling. He first moved there with his family in 1972 and bought the cottage sixteen years later in 1988, the year before he was elected the Oxford Professor of Poetry.[27] Then he used Glanmore as a place to write during the week and a place to gather with family at the weekend. Heaney always had time for his children as he wrote. Many of the letters are interrupted by a son or daughter coming to play or talk, an invitation he was happy to yield to. Heaney was a poet of approach, in landscape and in composition.

Driving to Glanmore took him south of his Sandymount home, the sea on his left, the low mountains on his right, the flat cap of the Sugar Loaf giving way to the green Wicklow valleys. The words Heaney associated with the place were 'flow' and 'lift', two standard motifs of his poetry and the substance of that lilting harmony, 'The Blackbird of Glanmore'. This is the last poem in *District and Circle*, but it calls back to a much earlier work of art from exactly the time of Heaney's transition to Glanmore, Edward McGuire's portrait of the poet from 1974. That painting now hangs in the Ulster Museum, which is testament to

---

[26] Saddlemyer bought the cottage in 1971 from the Yeats scholar A. N. Jeffares. The estate it was built on has a connection in turn to the Synge family. The house is a constant presence through Heaney's letters, where it is documented first as a refuge and then a retreat.
[27] Heaney entered the election as a candidate thanks to the encouragement of the Irish academic and poet at Magdalen College, Bernard O'Donoghue. Heaney wrote of himself in this role as a 'Fifty-year old, smiling, self-doubting man'. To Margot and Donald Fanger, 18 May 1989, *LSH*.

the all-island reality of Heaney's life and art. Heaney sits at a table in it, square on but for the feet, which turn towards each other, shyly. Before him is an open book, behind him a recessed window half the painting tall, rich with buds and green leaves, among which are three birds, two of them juvenile blackbirds. McGuire's painting is an allegory of becoming, in keeping with Heaney's life at the time, and with Glanmore, the province of birds and fields. That open view is crowded out in the poem, as if it has not resolved yet into shape. Heaney's life in McGuire's painting is in process, the lines of the wood floor running up through the threads of his trousers to his jumper and echoed in the wave of his hair. That flow and lift has its refrain in 'The Blackbird of Glanmore', a song hedged in otherwise by memory. The poem begins and ends with the blackbird watching Heaney as he comes and goes from Glanmore. Its middle sections recall the poet's dead brother and father, the whole an act of translation between sound and place.

> On the grass when I arrive,
> Filling the stillness with life,
> But ready to scare off
> At the very first wrong move.
> In the ivy when I leave.
> It's you, blackbird, I love.[28]

Glanmore is a place of pause, a portal for the poet between his lived and his writing life. The sentinels of that place are the dead, and in this, the blackbird can be mistaken for an omen, as one of his neighbours did when his younger brother died. The sense of augury reminds Heaney of his version of Sophocles' *Philoctetes*, *The Cure at Troy*, in which he imagined the call of death to the living as signal of an overwhelming grief. The reverie is broken by the car lock closing, the heavy sound spooking the bird and giving Heaney

---

[28] 'The Blackbird of Glanmore', *DC*.

a bird's eye view of myself,
A shadow on raked gravel
In front of my house of life.[29]

This was Glanmore to Heaney, a place perched between the under- and the overworld, the past and the present, the future a shadow given shape by the poet's careful landscaping, the raked gravel a zen garden in which life and death, might be faced. As Heaney leaves, the blackbird has taken to the ivy, a dense dark green like the background to McGuire's painting all those years ago, the younger man now older but familiar with loss all the same. The grounds of Glanmore are in this poem again like the precincts of Epidaurus, a theatre in which time and experience find form in words of place and life. Glanmore was both a retreat and an extension, all the more so after the Heaney family moved into the south Dublin suburb of Sandymount, close to the curving bay that arcs towards Dun Laoghaire, the city air giving way to salt and ozone. There, his study was at the top of the house, like a nest in the roof until Marie ordered skylights in. Then, 'extravagant Sky entered and held surprise wide open.'[30] The idea is of a kind with much of Heaney's larger landscapes. Composed in darkness, they opened slowly to a brighter light, the illumination of which signified a change as much in his way of looking as in what he looked at. The process between was a synthetic act of reading, writing, and living, a social geometry that summoned even the same places in Heaney's poetry in various forms.

Heaney's landscapes then were portals of place and time, the contexts for which the first visible specifics can obscure. Many of his poems of the north, for example, were written in the south, or inflected by experiences further away again, as so often with America. Heaney thought about these transits deeply, as when he met the Belfast-born novelist Brian Moore in California.[31] Moore is best known now for his novel *The Emperor of Ice*

---

[29] Ibid. [30] 'The Skylight', *ST*.
[31] Brian Moore (1921–1999) was born in Belfast and emigrated to Canada in 1948, before moving to California in 1966. Three of his novels were nominated for the Booker Prize, and he wrote numerous screenplays. Heaney read Moore's novels when Heaney was a young teacher in Belfast in the 1960s, before the two met in California in the early 1970s. Heaney wrote an obituary for Moore in which he said 'my abiding memory of him is a lovely kindness, a smile

Cream, but he had a successful career as a scriptwriter in Hollywood, and Heaney visited him during one of his earliest visits to America when Heaney held a visiting teaching position at Berkeley from 1970. The windy sands of Malibu were unexpectedly familiar to Heaney, as was the sense of fraternity with another northerner far from home. As so many poems show, Heaney's sense of place was elastic and deeply connected to his restlessness, which figures in constant images of motion. There is rarely a poem that sits still, no matter that the poet longed in his private mind for the peace of Glanmore or his Sandymount attic, up the narrow stairs to a desk by the high window. All of which is to say that landscape is a term to acknowledge the breadth of Heaney's ideas of place, informed as they were by the irregularities of time and experience. It is a thought to keep in mind as the late poems return to waymarkers familiar from the beginning, especially in the townlands around Bellaghy, the poetic grounds for which change subtly, and often fundamentally, over time.

For now, many of the significant places in Heaney's poetry are still accessible. The walk out by Church Island leads through sedgy farmland that is a refuge for meadow pipits, in disastrous decline elsewhere with the loss of habitats due to the planting of winter cereals. Territory of the red squirrel, fox, and badger, the margins of field and river are home to seasonal migrants from the far north, whooper swans and geese. The surface idyll is misleading given the apparition of algal blooms in Lough Neagh. The sources of this pollution lie in intensive agriculture and under-regulation, the roots of which go back even into Heaney's childhood. The poem 'Moyulla' describes his early impressions of the river, which include the white froth pumped out from a nearby factory that made condensed milk there from the 1940s to the 1970s. Heaney's awareness of this is not environmental in the sense that the poem does not connect the change in water quality with industrial pollution. But it does observe a change that is one of a series in land use and farming practice, all of which have brought the wider ecology of the Lough to its present state of near collapse. It may be the case that much of all writing up to now will look like this in retrospect,

and a wisecrack, the complete Belfast combination of downbeat and upfront, a *reductio* not *ad absurdem* but *ad veritatem*.' Seamus Heaney, 'Brian Moore', *The Harp* (15: 2000), 122–3.

memorial to the necropolis of the earth that future generations will inherit. It may even be that Heaney's rains and mists will lose the impression of subtle approach they suggest to the deepest questions of suffering and healing. In a world of driving storms and fires, how will Heaney's gentle departures be read, if books are still there to be read at all?

Late Heaney is in this sense an art of the ecological end times, his life and poetry a span from the pre- to the post-historic, the present but the briefest moment of significant connection. If anything, this brings a new charge to Heaney's connection with the plants, animals, and objects he encounters in his landscapes, which become a provisional assembly of endangered presences in contradiction of their significance as symbols of the previous, enduring world. The ghost of this awareness is in 'Sonnets from Hellas', which accompanies the Heaneys' journey west from Athens, stopping for petrol to see

> ...the goatherd
> With his goats in the forecourt of the filling station,
> Subsisting beyond eclogue and translation.[32]

In received historical time, the scene suggests a persistence of culture, beyond the self-conscious. In the Anthropocene, it suggests a series of disjunctions, the unevenness of fossil-fuelled development pitched against the practice of subsistence agriculture, the methods of which might signal what remains of our collective future as much as it does of our far past.[33] The significance of this for the construction and symbolism of Heaney's landscapes is the degree to which the poems are aware of the irregularity of the natural world, historically and environmentally. From the earliest work, he had a sense of the connection between the earth and human disturbance, the ripples of which he followed out from the puddles beneath the farmyard pump. The deep layers of colonial distortion are everywhere in the poetry, like geology, the spurs of which

---

[32] 'Sonnets from Hellas', *EL*.
[33] The Anthropocene is a term commonly used to describe that period during which humans have had a substantial impact on the environment of the planet.

Heaney discovered in the work of the archaeologist P. V. Glob.[34] The step from here to the recognition that earth, river, and sky were finite resources of human extraction is less well documented in the poetry, except in those moments when a landscape is threatened by violent change in its stewardship.

The consequence of this is that more than the specific subjects of the poetry, the forms and language are adequate to the present moment of environmental crisis. The closely bound histories of colonialism and the extraction of natural resources are well documented, and connected intimately too to the present state of Lough Neagh, since the ownership of its bed and banks resides in the hands of the Earl of Shaftesbury, an English aristocrat who lives in Devon. The environmental impact of this possession includes dredging of the Lough bed for sand used in roadworks and building, which has in turn diminished fish and bird life. Such industry hums in the background of the poems even as its frontiers pushed closer to his imaginative territory with the construction of the new road between Castledawson and Toome, which cuts right through the quiet evening landscapes of the Bann's beginnings. This is the true heartland of Heaney's poetry, a territory that stretched across time and place, its 'oozy sand' a pathway to Dante as to the riverbank.

Close by is Lough Neagh Fishermen's Co-operative, where eels are harvested on their return after long journeys abroad. The site has the air of a barracks, the mouth of the river braced by rusting metal for the operation of the catch. The place is much favoured by nesting herons, whose voices are often the only sound to be heard above the run of the water and the distant traffic. Toome used to be a bottleneck on the road from Derry to Belfast, before the bypass cut through the lowlands of the Bann. It was not unlike building a motorway through Grasmere, never mind the effect on the migrating geese who rest and feed in the wet fields the new road rumbles through. Among its unintended consequences is the cutting off of places that were in Heaney's childhood from their current access, as happened with the Lagans Road. Toome's later

---

[34] Faber published *The Bog People* in 1969. Heaney wrote to Charles Monteith from Berkeley in 1971 that the 'new Glob (lovely name) book came yesterday', 5 May 1971, *LSH*. Heaney soon joked that such was his influence, Glob would come looking for royalties.

air of desolation is partly a legacy of the Troubles and of the subsequent development of infrastructure projects, both of which add obscuring layers over the landscape as Heaney knew or remembered it. The Troubles, of course, were their own kind of infrastructure project, the edge of the town shadowed by the high brick wall and wire fence of the police station. The friction between the installation and the local population was a kind of electricity Heaney picked up on, the 'negative ions'[35] that register in the poetry of that place. Toome, like Bellaghy, had a particular charge, both historical and present, which linked a folk memory of the 1798 rebellion to the trauma of the hunger strikes.[36] Heaney followed the funerals from Dublin and corresponded with close friends about the significance of each moment that left another mark in a landscape already deeply scarred.

The question remains of what relationship there exists between these complex and ongoing histories, the social life of an individual and a community, which often extends far beyond the particulars of any single place or time, and the writing of poetry. Landscape is in this sense the conditional composition of a view from one place and time over many others. The details are important but not determinant since the perspective changes according to the moment. Constituent of all are the forms and rhythms that set this stage, the words, images, and ideas that give shape over time to a scene that becomes a panorama, a second that becomes significant, an impression that deepens into a landscape. In poetry, the picture is a form of words, drawn together as a painter might assemble a palette from the suggestion of light and shade. Heaney did this with intent, much as he evolved his practice from his early to his late work. The transition might be imagined as a clearing in the weather given the fogs and rain of the first work, the wet and squelch of a bog land that offered depth with a preset perspective. That fatalism generated some of the most negative responses Heaney received to his poetry, as if he had given in to violence. Later he looked up for longer, the light in the sky growing from the once-in-a-lifetime light of a passing comet

---

[35] 'At Toomebridge', *EL*.
[36] Heaney knew the families of two dead hunger strikers, Francis Hughes and Thomas McElwee. He attended McElwee's wake, an event recorded in the poem 'The Wood Road'. All three are now buried in the cemetery of St Mary's church, Bellaghy.

to a wider illumination, which in the end lingered even after death. This enlightenment was the gathering of much reading, experience, and travel, the older Heaney visiting Greece, translating Virgil, and finding correspondence in Wordsworth and Rilke.

Everywhere then there are images of leaving and return, however the traveller is changed by the experience. The cycles of country life are measured increasingly in the lough water, the river and sky, as much as they are in the immediate territory of fields and farms. Heaney was alive to all this from the beginning and understood its apparition as the tuning in to a frequency, poetry a clearance of distortion. As a child, the family sofa was a train or a gondola, on which the children perched, listening to the radio. The wire to the aerial ran into the house from a tree outside and

> When it moved in wind,
> The sway of language and its furtherings
> Swept and swayed in us like nets in water[37]

The catch in Heaney's poetry is its depth. The work is so full of familiar things the temptation is to think of them immediately as comfortable, and given. Sometimes they are, and in the later poems, this is sometimes evidence of the poet performing a certain version of himself, which at its worst came close to cliché. Otherwise, the world bends in the poems, its edges twisting and turning, blurring and bending, the poet like the child, trawling the nets of perception in the depths, hoping to catch signs and suggestions. This practice is constant throughout Heaney's poetry, from early to late. It evolved over time towards a gathering of frequencies, which is different from the intense, visionary moments of many of the poems written at the height of the Troubles. Then, the speaker was close to being overwhelmed by the violent rush of the past into the present. Later, the speaker creates a landscape in which the past and present overlap and take form in living nature. 'At Toomebridge' describes this change in terms that read like a proclamation:

---

[37] 'A Sofa in the Forties', *SL*.

Where the flat water
Came pouring over the weir out of Lough Neagh
As if it had reached an edge of the flat earth
And fallen shining to the continuous
Present of the Bann.
   Where the checkpoint used to be.
   Where the rebel boy was hanged in '98.
   Where negative ions in the open air
   Are poetry to me. As once before
   The slime and silver of the fattened eel.[38]

Heaney liked to say that he lived as a child in a prehistorical society, by which he meant partly that the chronologies of the industrial and globalized world did not yet apply to a culture rooted still in repetitive and established practices of language, belief, and social association. There is a suggestion of the idea in his description of the mouth of the Bann as a flat land and river, as if there was some drop off beyond the horizon. The effect is to create a screen of the sky. Vertical before the reader is a flicker of insurgent memory, rural County Derry a place of resistance and surveillance. The charge of the air generates its own electric light, which the poet summons before he dives for the depths again. Eels are one of Heaney's old familiars, most importantly in 'Station Island', when the ghost of James Joyce instructs him to strike out and search for 'elver-gleams in the dark of the whole sea'.[39] Their skin is the substance of strange sensation, and their travels like that of the poet, oceanic, transcontinental, long gone and longing for home.

Back from the lough shore, Heaney more often thought of the physical landscape as enclosure. As often with the later poetry, this is a consequence of reading and history, as well as of place and the imagination. He was aware from early on of the checkpoints and the military. The American build-up before the liberation of Europe made a deep impression on the young child, as did the uneven interaction between the bureaucracy of the state of Northern Ireland and its subjects. He was

[38] 'At Toomebridge', *EL*.   [39] 'Station Island XII', *SI*.

aware too of the colonial history of the north as plantation and expulsion. Unsure of how to proceed as a younger poet, Heaney sided with the defeated of the past. His metaphorical association between Irish irregular soldiers of the sixteenth century and himself as a poet is branched by images of woods, trees, and hidden places. The lip at the edge of this world has more solid form, as in a poem like 'Polish Sleepers', which is a poem of childhood, and of summer. More than that, the poem is a rare moment of parchedness in Heaney's work, comparable only to a poem like 'Westering', which ends in the dry dust of the distant moon. 'Polish Sleepers' is more immediate and organic and has about it a sense of the half-awake.

> A moulded verge, half-skirting, half-stockade,
> Soon fringed with hardy ground-cover and grass.
> But as that bulwark bleached in sun and rain
> And the washed gravel pathway showed no stain,
> Under its parched riverbed
> Flinch and crunch I imagined tarry pus
> Accruing, bearing forward to the garden
> Wafts of what conspired when I'd lie
> Listening for the goods from Castledawson…
> Each languid, clanking waggon,
> And afterwards, *rust, thistles, silence, sky*.[40]

One pleasure of the late poems is the fact that they become landscapes themselves, images from the earlier work regathered in poems open to new elements. Constant are the basic building blocks, the words and images that are there from the beginning and that last to the end. Sometimes in these late poems, the formation of the old and new leads to the over-familiar phrase. Sometimes the reader has a sense of the words being gathered for the sake of it, with nothing of the spark that makes the real poems light. 'Polish Sleepers' tacks between the two, as in that clatter of hyphenated words in the first lines. These are gestures towards the linguistic territory of the north that Heaney explored

[40] 'Polish Sleepers', *DC*.

through his fascination with Iron Age and Viking culture. His version of *Beowulf* was testament to this long-held interest. So was his habit of using compound words to describe singular objects, which sometimes gives the later poems a feeling of delay, as if the poem is talking around something and not to it. Beside this, there are words that echo with the reader from decades before. Stockade is a relic from 'Exposure', the riverbed a hint from 'North'. Together they suggest a speaker solitary and open to experience. Previously that experience was political and personally felt. Later, it is sensuous and dreamy. In 'Exposure', the poem wanders between winter trees dripping with rain. In 'Polish Sleepers', time has thickened into 'tarry pus', the creosote binding of the railway tracks carrying over the air with the sound of the slow train. Pus suggests infection, and stains the poem with unease. It has its corollary of decay in 'rust' and together they locate the poem in several times and places. The co-ordinates to discover them are the last four italicized words, '*rust, thistles, silence, sky*'. These allude to a poem by Czeslaw Milosz called 'The Thistle, the Nettle', which imagines a future world without human language.

> Who shall I be for men many generations later?
> When, after the clamour of tongues, the award goes to silence?
>
> I was to be redeemed by the gift of arranging words
> But must be prepared for an earth without grammar.
>
> For the thistle, the nettle, the burdock, the belladonna,
> And a small wind above them, a sleepy cloud, silence.

This still leaves unexamined the other layer of associations in the Heaney poem, which is the association between Poland and the railway sleepers. Milosz is a waypoint in this journey, which returns the reader to the unease of pus and rust. It expands too our awareness of both the Heaney and the Milosz poems' ecologies, rooted as they are in weeds, those flowers diminished only by human category. The enclosures of Heaney's poem take on another, ghastly, aspect as when the description of how the railway sleepers are laid out repeats the way wood was piled for the crematoria of the concentration camps. That history is laid deeply in the poem, and not readily apparent. It points to the new shape of old questions in Heaney's poetry, which is the drawing of a landscape as a theatre in which the poem asks could it, and should it, have done more? The lazy airs of the Castledawson train carry with them the accusation that the poet is too detached. But it suggests too that the landscape of these poems outlasts the atrocities they witness.

This returns us to the necessity of rural Co. Derry to Heaney's global view. Mutable, motive and mnemonic, it is itself, given, inherited and familiar, and it is other, shifting, deep and open to all kinds of connections. The late poems manage these transitions with organic complexity, the weave of established words and images overlaid with the perspective of age and failing health. The imagination of landscape in poetry describes a method of engaging with the world's contours sensually and ethically. The historical landmarks of this poetic territory were often barbarous, memorials to holocaust, oppression, and civil war. Instead of joining them in one stony litany, Heaney made the ground boggy and uncertain, as if in giving the speaker a place to hide the poem gives the reader room to reflect, and survive. This is what Heaney called the murderous and the marvellous, and it is the substance of much of his place-writing, which is in turn the landscape of his ethical thought.

At the heart of all this were the family and friendships that Heaney maintained throughout his life. If he imagined the role of the poet as a solitary affair, he wrote poetry that was social and intimate. The later work has less reserve and more playfulness in its social imagination, even as it remains constant in its attention to the worst that humanity has done. The full range of this register can be read in Heaney's poem for his artist friend Sonja Landweer, 'To a Dutch Potter in Ireland'. They had exhibited together, and one genesis of the poem is the physical impression that Landweer's pottery made on him when he saw them in her studio. Another dimension of Heaney's poetry is the way in which it sees earth, water, and light in physical objects, as if landscape was carried into art in the substance of its constitution. Pottery is an art of clay and water, physical, visual, and turned by hand. Heaney was concerned with handmade things throughout his life. Whereas in the earlier work this could signal a distance between the poet and the people around him, in the later, this becomes the fabric of social association, pottery, like poetry, a hand-made summons of the elements into some shape significant to the imagination. The internal life of the external world is part of the late Heaney's divination of suffering, memory, and restitution. He wrote 'To a Dutch Potter in Ireland' as the first Gulf War was fought, and the haze of world conflict hangs over the first section of the poem like infernal shadow. This planetary aspect is a deep layer of the later poetry and suggests how Heaney's drawing of landscape became more imagistic and associative as the sediments of his work shifted and stirred at the turn of a century that seemed to promise better. 'To a Dutch Potter in Ireland' has a preface and three sections, the preface setting the terms by which to read what follows:

> *Then I entered a strongroom of vocabulary*
> *Where words like urns that had come through the fire*
> *Stood in their bone-dry alcoves next a kiln*[41]

In this view, the poem is a gallery into which the poet will place the right objects in the right order. These objects come marked with their own histories, and the poet's responsibility, in Heaney's telling, is their installation in a proper moral order. That order survives under threat, and partly the poem is a refuge for these symmetries in face of the worst atrocity. It is unruly too, erotic and submerged, a channel of energies that Heaney associated with the basic forms of his poetic landscape. The first section begins:

> The soils I knew ran dirty. River sand
> Was the one clean thing that stayed itself
> In that slabbery, clabbery, wintry, puddled ground.
> Until I found Bann clay.[42]

The rivers that run through Heaney's poetry are of the substance of their composition. They represent the distance between the known and the unknown, from one bank unto the other, and also the depths of the

---

[41] 'To a Dutch Potter in Ireland', *SL*.   [42] Ibid.

imagination, and its flow. They host an ecology, of eels, fish, and birds that give the greater landscape its miniature, interconnected life. They feed the larger bodies of water too, loughs, seas, and oceans that represent depths from which only echoes return. Landweer is a figure of water, lit by nature:

> ...swimming in the sea
> Or running from it, luminous with plankton,
> A nymph of phosphor by the Norder Zee...[43]

In contrast, the times were fired by war and occupation, which Landweer survived like pottery in the kiln. This is not, however, a poetry of progression, as if water and fire are in simple sequence. Instead, there are elements of each in the other. Landscape in the poetry is a holding of these divergent and often terrible forces together, a dramatization of what has and can happen before a reader who is never allowed to think anything is over, or foreclosed. Just as the sea shines with phosphorescent light, so the burning land can be soothed by 'clean sand and kaolin', '"now that the rye crop waves beside the ruins"'.[44] The image of the field as sea comes from Heaney's translation of the Dutch poet J. C. Bloem and is a brief signal of correspondence between the global and the local, the terrible and the intimate. The poem's second section begins with a clarity that is reminiscent of earlier moments in 'Station Island', now without the personal exhaustion. In this later work, the poet is further from the scene, observant still but not bloodied, muddied, and tired as so often before. This distance invites a different rhythm to the poem, which is another step towards the later 'Human Chain'. Continuing is the mixed imagery of land and water, the light of spring all 'pearly clarity'.[45] Familiar too is the turn in the last stanzas to give advice. Earlier that advice was oblique and inward looking. Now it is general and prescriptive, which can make of a poem a damp squib.

---

[43] Ibid.   [44] Ibid.   [45] Ibid.

> To have lived it through and now be free to give
> Utterance, body and soul—to wake and know
> Every time that it's gone and gone for good, the thing
> That nearly broke you—
>
> Is worth it all, the five years on the rack,
> The fighting back, the being resigned, and not
> One of the unborn will appreciate
> Freedom like this ever.⁴⁶

Still, the words echo with their earlier selves, 'freedom' read in the voice of 'The Tollund Man', the violence of northern Europe a symbolic inheritance as persistent as 'the everlasting sky'. If the horizon of this stalemate was all air and distance, in mitigation, Heaney returned to the mixed media of earth and sea to make freedom from violence a felt reality. Death remained, but held now in natural pattern and detached from human practice. As nature takes on human form, so does the body find form in the rhythms of land- and seascape. This metamorphosis is reflected in Heaney's interest in writing versions of poems from other languages, as he began to do more and more with Virgil. In the closing sequence of 'To a Dutch Potter in Ireland', Heaney looks to the Dutch of J. C. Bloem for a model of synchronicity between nature and survival.⁴⁷

> Turning tides, their regularities!
> What is the heart, that it ever was afraid,
> Knowing as it must know spring's release,
> Shining heart, heart constant as a tide?⁴⁸

The rise and fall of the waters illuminates one more condition, which is very much of the late poetry, and that is the quality of light. Much of the earlier work is dressed in the rain and dark, the late flukes of wet autumn leaves, the black of night by Lough Derg, but not so the later. The illumination of the later poems has a wide range of affect and is often in

---

⁴⁶ Ibid.
⁴⁷ J. C. Bloem (1887–1966) was a Dutch poet whose 'After Liberation' became a celebrated expression of freedom after the end of the German occupation in World War Two.
⁴⁸ 'To a Dutch Potter in Ireland', *SL*.

response to the work of other artists, from Landweer and Bloem to the painter Barrie Cooke. The grammar that governs these luminary declensions takes shape in these last books from the work of Virgil, who is a constant presence. The Roman poet had been audible to Heaney for a long time before he was captivated by David Ferry's translation of the *Eclogues*.[49] The *Aeneid* plays an important part in Brian Friel's *Translations*, for instance, the founding of a future city from the ruins of the present a powerful theme for communities fractured by violence and language loss.[50] Heaney certainly read Virgil as a contemporary, hedged in local speech and image. For all that, the local has shifted, from the intimacies of Anahorish to the broader vale of the Bann river valley, the tributary points of Toome, Bellaghy, and Magherafelt gathered into a lyric landscape that is at once literary and social. 'Bann Valley Eclogue' draws this new place in old and braided form, the history of dispossession and resistance woven into a poetry of landscape and memorial, the hedgerows leading at last to the hedge-school master, late Heaney absorbed of all his lessons, the poet become a place, the place a poem.

> Bann Valley Muses, give us a song worth singing,
> Something that rises like the curtain in
> Those words *And it came to pass* or *In the beginning*.[51]

Virgil is augur here, and inauguration, less a model than a waymarker. Heaney had prepared for the long foray for decades previous, his journey shadowed by death and war. Arrival at the idea of the Bann Valley offered more than respite. It was a looping together of words and themes

---

[49] 'David Ferry did a new translation of Virgil's *Eclogues*, published with the parallel Latin text, and for a while I was captivated entirely... Here was a young poet coming back with an almost vindictive artistry against the actual conditions of the times. There was something recognizable at work, a kind of Muldoonish resistance.' *SS*, 389.

[50] Heaney was intimately aware of Friel's dramatic project, which was itself underpinned by their collective endeavour in Field Day. He thought the play 'deeply conceived' in the conceit that it is spoken in English, but imagined in Irish, a boundary evident to the characters and so to the audience. *Translations* was first staged at the Guild Hall in Derry in 1981, the theatre programme containing two of Heaney's own translations from Irish into English. To Brian Friel, 26 November 1979, *LSH*.

[51] 'Bann Valley Eclogue', *EL*.

that had governed the poetry into new shapes, the contours of which can be read in this newly lit place. The sense of summary is clear enough from the figure of Virgil's first response:

> Here are my words you'll have to find a place for:
> *Carmen, ordo, nascitur, saeculum, gens.*
> Their gist in your tongue and province should be clear
> Even at this stage. Poetry, order, the times,
> The nation, wrong and renewal, then an infant birth
> And a flooding away of all the old miasma.[52]

'Bann Valley Eclogue' is a poem in flood, the old images of blood and waste washed away in the river's uprising, and with it the past's poison air. This new world is held together by root and flower, weeds in harmony with hay bales, the old division of crop and tare undone. It is a geography governed by patience and flow, the regular rhythms of field work a preparation for a peace that has finally arrived, the valley 'washed' like a 'new baby'.[53] This is a signature contentment across Heaney's later landscapes, their season summer, their model the Mediterranean world that shaped his late mind, poetry, and belief. The darkness of the earlier poems is still there, but further away, like a memory of winter in the brighter days. In these late works, brightness is a season, the summer light longer lasting than before. It passes, too, but in a drowsiness that suspends anxiety. The bounty of a poem like the related 'Glanmore Eclogue' is its 'baled hay and blackberries',[54] the sentences a storehouse of sensation. The old ghosts of past troubles remain in references to tenants and empire, but the presiding senses are pleasure and relief.

On winning the Nobel Prize, Heaney had remarked that he learned in middle age to look up instead of down, to wear his burdens more lightly, if not to set them aside. The pitch of these late poems is elevation, the flight of a kite or the raised voice of song, the pastoral become a ballad that is a hymn to the earth and sky as they are, now. The 'Glanmore Eclogue' asks this of the poet:

---

[52] Ibid.   [53] Ibid.   [54] Ibid.

A house and ground. And your own bay tree as well
And time to yourself. You've landed on your feet.
If you can't write now, when will you ever write?[55]

He answers that:

I have this summer song for the glen and you:
Early summer, cuckoo cuckoos,
Welcome, summer is what he sings.
Heather breathes on soft bog-pillows.
Bog-cotton bows to moorland wind.
The deer's heart skips a beat; he startles.
The sea's tide fills, it rests, it runs.
Season of the drowsy ocean…
The lark sings out his clear tidings.
Summer, shimmer, perfect days.[56]

These late landscapes are woven with new words that thread together in an old technique. As a reader, the first impression is of the turns between the fricative sounds of the northern voice and the liquid landscapes it describes, of bog and lough, and sea and river. Next, there is the awareness of volume, the poems breathing with the wind, the open sky a raised ceiling. Last is the sense of leave-taking, the poem a painting framed for the reader, more image, less idea. The 'Glanmore Eclogue' is of a kind with its predecessors, with its echoes of *Sweeney Astray* and its flirtation with the compound word forms that sometimes tend to self-parody.[57] But it is a finished work in the way that many of the earlier poems are not, the reader left in a scene the artist has departed from. Heaney veils this leave-taking in the easy forms of conversation, which is another reason why the

---

[55] 'Glanmore Eclogue', *EL*.   [56] Ibid.
[57] Heaney published his translation of *Buile Shuibhne* as *Sweeney Astray* in 1983. He began it a decade before in his first year at Glanmore, first attracted by the extracts he read in Kenneth Hurlstone Jackson's *A Celtic Miscellany*, which led him in turn to the Irish Texts edition and the idea to work on it himself. The original story tells of the madness of Suibhne mac Colmáin, king of the Dál nAraidi, after he was cursed by a saint. Heaney loved Sweeney's flight, and the figure of the displaced traveller with a sense for the elements resonates throughout his work. *SS*, 151–5.

back-and-forth of the eclogue suits his late self so well. In these poems, all memories are landscapes, all observations a point of view that the poet assembles from past journeys, past places. It is strange in the immediate sense to meet the past in the sunlight of early summer. Certainly, the poet was aware in his last collections that his time as a writer was shortening. Landscape endures through art that summons it, and Heaney's resource as a poet was to weave together the memories, experiences, and readings of his life into a mental territory that stretched from Attica to Derry. We will think later about the ghosts that inhabited this place, from the writers Heaney read, met, and imagined, to his family and friends. For now, let us think of Heaney's later landscapes as sensory forms of historical depth, shaped by his memory and his method, place a thick surface through which time shimmers.

Like much of Heaney's work, this late style is a deepening of what came before. 'Station Island' has a similar construction, historical shapes emerging from the disorienting gloom of pilgrimage. That sequence lacks the luminosity of the pastorals, where even in darkness there is light. There is a clarity too, which was denied his earlier speakers. There is heaven and hell now, and less purgatory, the skew towards salvation secured by the late speaker's generosity. Pilgrimage remains, but as enlightened progress between past and present, the fog of uncertainty lifted. Heaney spoke to this in his Nobel speech when he determined to raise his eyes skyward for inspiration. He practiced it after in 'The Little Canticles of Asturia', which imagines a journey on the Camino de Santiago in northern Spain.[58] A canticle is a hymn or chant, and each verse is a summons through language of sensations associated with spiritual progress. In the earlier poems, Heaney was concerned with seeing Ireland in another dimension. In the later, he has struck offshore and landed on new ground, which looks different for the journey. The drama is played out in the progress of this poem, which begins in 'the burning valley of Gijon'.[59] The night works of oil refineries give the landscape a

---

[58] Heaney wrote to Ted Hughes of his experience visiting Santiago de Compostela in the summer of 1996, the stonework and the spectacle 'just enough...to make you feel the huge collapse that has taken place at the centre of the Christian thing'. To Ted Hughes, 8 July 1996, *LSH*.
[59] 'The Little Canticles of Asturias', *EL*.

hellish aspect, which almost takes the poem back to Derry and the memory of a lighting fire in the home place. It was common once to hold the double pages of a newspaper across the open hearth so that a starting fire would take. The trick was to remove the paper before it went up too, the black and white singed to a crisp brown.

The idea rises in the poem as the valley deepens, the first verse a trial of memory and experience. It has its analogue in Heaney's long-standing fascination with Dante, the first verse a test, an entry, and an escape, as 'we lost all hope of reading the map right/ And gathered speed and cursed the hellish roads'.[60] Heaney writes at speed now, the slower circuits of Lough Derg accelerated to a compact verse. There is impatience here, but also joy, and freedom. This is the liberation of the late poems, their landscapes drawn in swift sweeps that have depth because the reader remembers the contrast with the earlier journeys, the earlier forms. The second verse has this quality, mindful as it is of a scene like 'The Seed Cutters', which imagined Heaney's rural past as a canvas equivalent to that painted by the Flemish master, Pieter Bruegel the Elder.[61] Then he saw continuity. Now difference has emerged. Beside the road to Piedras Blancas, the speaker sees men cutting 'aftergrass with scythes'.[62] It reminds him of 'home ground',[63]

> The Gaeltacht, say, in the nineteen-fifties,
> Where I was welcome, but of small concern
> To families at work in the roadside fields
> Who'd watch and wave at me from their other world[64]

The Irish language was always present in Heaney's poetry, not least in his fascination with the declensions of English between local place names and their social meaning, the distance between which his imagination visited. The Donegal Gaeltacht came back to him later, particularly in his memories of driving north and west with friends over the

---

[60] Ibid.
[61] Pieter Bruegel the Elder (c.1525–1569) was a Flemish artist. Heaney used *The Harvesters* (1565) as a model for 'The Seed Cutters', and referred to the painter as 'Breughel'.
[62] 'The Little Canticles of Asturias', *EL*.   [63] Ibid.   [64] Ibid.

years. 'Loughanure' is the best example of this, the poem a memorial for the painter Colin Middleton, whose own shimmering land- and seascapes are resonant with Heaney's poems of place and vision.[65] The poem takes its title from Middleton's painting of Loughanure, which is the Anglicized form of the Irish for lake of the yew. That painting now hangs under a slant of the ceiling in Heaney's home in Sandymount. It is darkly drawn, the stony foreground of a stacked wall giving way to the hint of water and a glimpse of Errigal in the distance, the lonely snow-capped mountain echoed in the drift of whitewashed houses that ridge the horizon. The view is still there today, down the lane by the angling club, just past the filling station. The painting had other anchors in Heaney's mind. The lake of the yew brings to mind that other yew lined water margin of the north, around Lough Beg, while Rannafast, the Irish-speaking district where Heaney summered as a child, is just a few miles seaward. The later poem suggests the difficulty of bringing this all together, the speaker passing through the west Donegal landscape and

> trying
> To remember the Greek word signifying
> A world restored completely[66]

Heaney often saw the rural, Irish-speaking past as a kind of Attica. The literary genealogy for this is in his reading and in his friendships, particular with Friel, whose plays worked similar ground. The transition in the later work is towards a resolution of meaning in landscape. Words become part of the sensory world, the boundary between the waving families and the travelling poet collapsed in the continuing present. The third and last canticle holds the scene together as never before.

> At San Juan de las Harenas
> It was a bright day of the body.
> Two rivers flowed together under sunlight.

---

[65] Colin Middleton (1910–1983) was a Belfast painter with a surreal flourish who Heaney first met in the early 1960s. That general scene is sketched in a letter to Heather Clark, 24 January 2000, *LSH*.
[66] 'Loughanure', *HC*.

Watercourses scored the level sand.
The sea hushed and glittered outside the bar.
And in the afternoon, gulls *in excelsis*
Bobbed and flashed on air like altar boys
With their quick turns and tapers and responses
In the great re-echoing cathedral gloom
Of distant Compostela, *stela, stela*.[67]

Heaney was always a little shy of embodiment, at least when it came to pleasure. The worn grooves of history are still visible in the scouring verb, but underwater now, and covered by the flow of two rivers. It is interesting to think of the flat surface of the Bann here from the Toome poems, in particular the way in which inland waters are so often a mirror and a stillness in the landscapes. Now that carries out into the bay, the sea quiet too, the only sound the seabirds, the poem written as a curve, the descent of the first verse risen in the last. What ended before in flames and darkness starts again now in chant and ritual, the sonic extent of which goes beyond the human, into bird and stone. The end of the verse is radiance, the presence of life a frequency felt through all the objects of the earth, a letting go that is not a goodbye to the world but an awareness of its unending dimensions. The stela is a gravestone and a refrain, a commemoration and a song made from the fabric of life, a composition that has its analogue in other, organic poems like 'Mint'. This begins unpromisingly, the mint a wild plant at the side of the house, 'almost beneath notice'.[68] Attention is love in the later work, sight, smell, and touch three securities of an existence that extends beyond them towards a solitariness that the later Heaney finds more and more in company of the natural world. The cycle of consciousness tends to run from memory to observation, attention and reflection, and from there to resignation, not as melancholy but a leaving, the living world departed from, but not over. 'Mint' ends like this too:

My last things will be first things slipping from me.
Yet let all things go free that have survived.

[67] 'The Little Canticles of Asturias', *EL*.   [68] 'Mint', *SL*.

> Let the smells of mint go heady and defenceless
> Like inmates liberated in that yard.
> Like the disregarded ones we turned against
> Because we'd failed them by our disregard.[69]

The last two lines are a graft on the poem's stem, and perhaps the weaker for it. There can be a tendency in the later books to surrender to rhymes and phrases that dilute the clarity of the speaker's observations. Still, that couplet of the letting go stands with any of Heaney's observations, and it is also the case that frequently in these poems a line or two, and sometimes a verse, exceed anything that came before. The whole works better in a poem like 'Human Chain', in which witness and the imagination merge in the motion of hand and lift. There is less too in that poem of accusation, although there is similar discomfort. The major issue that arises in all these landscapes of memory is the question of attitude, and bearing. Poise is a constant theme of Heaney's poetry and had been since he first thought about holding a pen, or digging a field. It continued to be so through his poems, his plays, and his versions, most lately in *Beowulf*, that epic of the Geats, its hero straight and true.

Heaney's deepest histories emerge from the uncertain ground between peace and war, in bog, and sea, and field. The whole is orchestrated in 'The Aerodrome', which brings flight, fight, and love together in a Derry panorama whose social form is intimate and felt. Where once there was a staginess in the relationship between poetry and experience, now there is suggestion, history a cross-hatch as Heaney puts it elsewhere, and landscape a sensation. The poem remembers the old airfield that serviced the American air force in its preparations for the liberation of Europe in World War Two.[70] This period made a deep mark in young Heaney's imagination and surfaces in many of his poems of childhood. On one of the roads I walk in summers out behind Magherafelt, there

---

[69] Ibid.
[70] The architectural remains of some of these installations can still be found in the townlands past Toome, towards Magherafelt. Belfast International Airport is on the site of the initial military airport near Lough Neagh, and four more followed. The Lough was used for torpedo practice, among other things, which speaks to the proximity of the north of Ireland to the Atlantic threat from U-boats, and to the general disregard of the Lough's ecological status.

are still remnants of this temporary occupation in sentry boxes now surrendered to wren and crow. The world rubs against this locality with some friction, Heaney calling the land 'usurped by a compulsory order',[71] the orders of the state always a form of removal. The poem is itself built on the remains of others, the echoes of Louis MacNeice's 'Meeting Point' barely audible in Heaney's light refrain.[72] In MacNeice,

> Time was away and somewhere else,
> There were two glasses and two chairs
> And two people with the one pulse[73]

In Heaney,

> No catchpenny stalls for us, no
> Awnings, bonnets, or beribboned gauds:
> Wherever the world was, we were somewhere else...'[74]

All literary landscapes bear the tares of other writers. Without them, the reader would find the path more difficult, the writer the lonelier way. Heaney had always thought carefully about the company he kept, in life and in literature. Thought adhered into a philosophy of action in 'Aerodrome', the last lines a set of observations that together have their own truth in place and time.

> If self is a location, so is love:
> Bearings taken, markings, cardinal points,
> Options, obstinacies, dug heels, and distance,
> Here and there and now and then, a stance.[75]

---

[71] 'The Aerodrome', *DC*.
[72] Louis MacNeice (1907–1963) was a poet and broadcaster, born in Belfast, who was then educated and lived in England. A friend and contemporary of Auden, he was an important figure for Derek Mahon and Edna and Michael Longley. Heaney was familiar with much of MacNeice's work and quoted from 'Meeting Point' in a letter to Roger Garfitt, 29 September 1983, *LSH*.
[73] Louis MacNeice, 'Meeting Point'.   [74] 'The Aerodrome', *DC*.   [75] Ibid.

Heaney took bearings throughout his life, and some of his most important co-ordinates were set in context of his friendship with other artists and writers. Now that we have drawn the landscapes of Heaney's later poetry, we will think in the next chapter about the paintings and books that shaped it, before we come to the people, living and dead, real and imagined, who move through it. We began this reading of landscape by the shores of Lough Neagh, finishing it in the overgrown fields of a long-gone summer. Before us are the shadow territories that shape the edges of this Heaney country, the artists and places that are sometimes layered into Derry, and are sometimes far beyond. Late as it is, the long days shorten, and with them, the poems change, illness and death weighed against friendship and consideration, the bearings set for a last time.

Late Heaney. Nicholas Allen, Oxford University Press. © Nicholas Allen 2026.
DOI: 10.1093/9780198985419.003.0002

3
Bearings

Seamus Heaney grew up in a landscape unusual even for the north of Ireland, the flatlands of Lough Neagh framed by the Sperrins' low shoulders, the plantation geography of centuries past still visible in the layout of ditch, field, river, and village, the staccato of Ulster Scots giving way to the soft inclinations of an English tempered by Irish and Latin, the deep language of place and belief. Driving the backroads from Bellaghy to Magherafelt, Draperstown, Moneymore, and back is to loop through histories whose sharp edges still cut the green sward of summer fields, the roads lined with flags, the kerbs newly painted, blood red and blue. For all that, there is a slow beauty to the place, resting by the lough shore, the river's edge. It took me years to see it, thinking of rural Derry, when I thought of it at all, as a place to pass through on the way to somewhere else. Now each summer I look forward to the hawthorn and the buzzards, the bog cotton and the silver of Lough Neagh, the inland sea around which the townlands gather.

One recent summer I did set out to find the Lagans Road, which no one I knew had heard of. I ended up circling round in my parents' car, driving up and down country lanes to no purpose except to puzzle a man out walking his dog. On the verge of giving up we stopped at a petrol station with used cars for sale. I followed my father in just as the woman behind the counter called her husband, from the back office, sure he'd know where we meant. The door opened and the man stopped, looked at my father and guldered, 'That man tortured me!' It turned out my father was the man's bank manager years ago, a relationship neither forgot. Lagans Road, meanwhile, had a changed name since Heaney wrote about it, and a different entrance behind the Thatch Inn, which now sits marooned above the new road that bisects Heaney's hinter wetlands. The shifting landscape is appropriate to the poem I had in mind, which imagines the ghost of Edward Thomas walking by.[1] The road is one of hundreds like it bar the high ditches and the old trees, which were there before Heaney, tall, broad and leafy with blossom on the warm day I passed by. The poem did not make the place, but it did make the road a place to stop, look, listen, and think about Heaney there, mindful of other times and places.

> He's not in view but I can hear a step
> On the grass-crowned road, the whip of daisy heads
> On the toes of boots.[2]

Out of sight is a pair of lovers, the memory of which prompts the thought of Thomas.

> Behind the hedge
> Eamon Murphy and Teresa Brennan—
> Fully clothed, strong-arming each other—
> Have sensed him and gone quiet. I keep on watching
> As they rise and go.
> And now the road is empty.
> Nothing but air and light between their love-nest
> And the bracken hillside where I lie alone.[3]

Heaney's intimate style veils the poem's mechanics, assembled as it is from bits of other poems, fragments of memory, and the constant pull in the late poems to create an atmosphere. 'Edward Thomas on the Lagans Road' is a study of how the buried and the past can become the floating and the future, the poem holding the two in mind like the line for a kite. The hint of Yeats in the rise and go is a gesture and a suggestion that Heaney has gone further, up out of the rag and bone shop towards the reconsideration of all things in open space.

---

[1] Edward Thomas (1878–1917) was a poet who died in World War One. One of Heaney's very last written poems, 'In a Field', was written in response to Thomas's poem, 'As the Team's Head-Brass'. Thomas was also a great influence on Michael Longley.
[2] 'Edward Thomas on the Lagans Road', DC.   [3] Ibid.

Utter evening, as it was in the beginning,
Until the remembered come and go of lovers
Brings on his long-legged self on the Lagans Road—
Edward Thomas in his khaki tunic[4]

World War Two is a regular presence in Heaney's poems, in part because so many American soldiers were stationed near Bellaghy during the preparation for the liberation of Europe, in part because of the influence of the radio on his childhood imagination, and in part in this poem thanks to the service of some of his neighbours in North Africa. Edward Thomas was long dead by then, killed by the explosion of a shell in 1917, which suggests again the ways in which Heaney's poems about other poets are panoramas of citation, suggestion, and dislocation, all of which suggests an attitude to art and life that settles in the late poems into rhythms of speech and movement. It is a deceptively simple method, in which a remembered life meets millennia of art in phrases of personal history that give bearing to the otherwise disconnected. Such poems are acts of restitution, observance, and pleasure too despite everything the poet had experienced in the north of Ireland. Steeped in Heaney's reading, they are measures of the use he found in other writers, travelling the distance from Thomas to Virgil by the shortcuts of local landscape and Derry talk.

The Roman is key to this late work, and features more as Heaney ages, Virgil a foreign guide to the familiar, a pastoral poet who heard the echo of politics in fields and rivers. Those echoes carried other voices with them, Heaney's versions of Virgil a gathering of the colonial energies that shaped the mental and physical landscape he wrote in. In 'Eclogue IX', Heaney shapes a conversation between two farmers, Moeris and Lycidas, who speak as if from Derry in the time of Caesar. Virgil opened the ground for Heaney to write of his late love for the Derry countryside in summer, and the eclogue is prelude to a last poem like 'The Riverbank Field.' Heaney shies away from that poem's run towards the afterlife in the Eclogue, the landscape not shaped yet for leaving. So Moeris asks,

[4] Ibid.

> What's in the sea and the waves that keeps you spellbound?
> Here earth breaks out in wildflowers, she rills and rolls
> The streams in waterweed, here poplars bend
> Where the bank is undermined and vines in thickets
> Are meshing shade with light. Come here to me.
> Let the mad white horses paw and pound the shore.[5]

The pattern of light and dark is mapped in the poem by the way marker 'here', the conversational tone of the eclogue an invitation for Heaney to speak through Virgil in his own voice, as is common across many of Heaney's translations of other works. The wavering images perch the poem in a falling moment, the surrender to which is the frenzy of that last line, which itself has an unusual source. Caught between the river and the country, empire and the sea, is Rudyard Kipling's 'White Horses', a poem that celebrated Britain's late nineteenth century imperial might.[6] Pitching the pastoral against the oceanic, Heaney works into the eclogue a local attitude that is mindful of the traumatic depths it traverses.

By the time the reader comes to the late poems, Heaney's art is a layered, echoing image scape, with traces of his earlier work throughout, and allusions from his own reading life. Heaney came to describe the attention to these energies in his poetry as a stance, as if the reader could stand in one position, listen, watch, and imagine a world of meaning that shifts with every change of that stance, as it must each time we read. The roots of this idea are various and can be felt in the tension of poems that weigh the pull of the world against the lightness of the air. Heaney had already voiced this concern in the poem 'Antaeus' in *North*. In classical mythology Antaeus's strength ebbed when his feet left the ground. To go too far was to lose all perspective. To stay too close was an abnegation. The line between was thin and mutable, and looked different in different places, and in different words. Threaded through all this

---

[5] 'Virgil: Eclogue IX', *EL*.
[6] Rudyard Kipling (1865–1936) was the laureate of the high period of the British Empire. His prose and poetry shaped generational attitudes to British possession of global territories. 'White Horses' combines the imagery of land and sea power with the violence of divine right: 'To bray your foeman's armies- / To chill and snap his sword-/ Trust ye the wild White Horses,/ The Horses of the Lord!' It is subversive to hear this echo in the mouth of Moeris, who has himself been dispossessed of his land.

is the natural fact of a world writer coming into the company of more and more people, an inescapable sociability that Heaney managed with professional grace. Behind this again is a self-measuring in context of all the artists who have come before, the poet wondering where in the end his words and his reputation will rest.

The first place was among 'The Bookcase'. Heaney was a keen reader, although his own bookshelves are as enigmatic as his private self. It is hard to tell from the list of his books now kept in Bellaghy which are of personal interest and which of obligation. There are clues in his personal library as to some of the sources he read in conjunction with the writing of his poems. There is Serena Vitale's study of the last months of Pushkin's life before his death in a duel and Mary McNeill's biography of the Belfast radical, Mary Ann McCracken. There is poetry and drama, from friends and contemporaries like Paul Muldoon and Michael Longley, local histories and scattered issues of the *Honest Ulsterman*. There are books on the poetry of Keats and of the Brontë sisters, books on modern art, folk song, and the Irish language. Together they say more about Heaney's eclectic interests, and his natural generosity, than they do about any relationship between his reading and his writing. Heaney was certainly committed to close reading when he wanted to explain something of another writer's work. He was conscious when he lectured in one university or another that he was in the company of professors who judged him for what he said, for which he had no desire to be found wanting.

For Heaney, then, 'The Bookcase' was a way to put shape on the variety, forms, and origins of his reading. It is a portal through which his own readers might find their own bearings, to strike out on their own. All journeys begin with the setting of coordinates. In 'The Bookcase' these are the elements of material and memory that frame the books themselves. The bookcase is made of ash or oak, two woods associated in his poetry with an older landscape, pre-plantation, ghosts of another language and society. It is made by hand and associated with the dedicated practice of the monk and the sailor, two figures frequently in Heaney's work and both symbolic of care and community. The wooden boards of the bookcase are like vellum, the relationship between page and writing organic and enduring. These qualities together are a primer for Heaney's writing at large. The books within are a kind of ballast, the stones around which the weight of the imagination settles to some form of equilibrium. There is Hugh MacDiarmid and Elizabeth Bishop, Yeats and Hardy, Frost and Stevens, paired off like rowers. The bookcase, like the sofa, is a medium to a collective consciousness to which the poem gives shape. By this late stage that collective consciousness is also made up of the relics of other poems by Heaney himself, 'Westering' a ghost and 'Human Chain' a premonition, the bookcase a work under construction. Both 'Westering' and 'Human Chain' are poems about gravity and weight. They speak to each other through 'The Bookcase' via Heaney's reading of Synge, whose play *Riders to the Sea* demands

> In the opening stage direction 'some new boards
> Standing by the wall,' and in Maurya's speech
> 'White boards' are like storm-gleams on the flood
>
> At the very end, or the salt salvaged makings
> Of a raft for books, a bier to be borne.
> I imagine us bracing ourselves for the first lift,
> Then staggering for balance, it has grown so light.[7]

As so often with Heaney's looping, intertwined art, the poem's end is in the poet's beginnings, 'The Bookcase' closing with a gesture back to Heaney's first collection, *Death of a Naturalist*, and another sea-blown poem, 'Synge on Aran'. On publication that early poem seemed like an obligation, one of many attempts by the post-revival generations to negotiate their place relative to Yeats and his contemporaries. In later context it seems more revealing of Heaney's abiding practice than a poem like 'Digging', a tool worn from overuse. With 'Synge on Aran' there is fatality too, and the sea, the wind, and the act of writing like

> a hard pen
> scraping in his head;
> the nib filled on a salt wind
> and dipped in the keening sea.[8]

[7] 'The Bookcase', *EL*.   [8] 'Synge on Aran', *DN*.

Heaney's elemental practice found its major form in the sequences he began to write in his second collection, *Door into the Dark*. Built into these chain poems of historical association were allusions to earlier canonical works of literature, as with Dante's *Inferno*.[9] Already then there was preparation of the idea that a longer poem divided into numbered sections could work individually as a scene of reflection, and collectively as a site of transformation. Added to this in the later poems is a pattern of the poet's own perspective; however, the poems still tend to deflection and distraction. In 'Aerodrome' the reader was invited to consider their relationship with life as they experienced it. In 'The Flight Path' the reader is summoned on the journey from the ground to the air and back, and invited at the end to take off themselves. That journey is personal to the poet, and self-revealing, dedicated as it is to Donald Davie.[10] But it is also literary, in ways that shape fundamentally the poem's bearing. 'The Flight Path' has six sections and was published in *The Spirit Level*, a collection that took its title from a line that signifies balance. The first part describes the speaker's memory of his father making a paper boat to give to his son. The imagery heals a break that Heaney made in his earliest poems between manual and imaginative labour. Gone are the guns, pens, and shovels, given way to the intricate folds of paper, much to the child's delight.

> A dove rose in my breast
> Every time my father's hands came clean
> With a paper boat between them, ark in air,
> The lines of it as taut as a pegged tent[11]

The first image that comes to mind in these lines is Noah's ark, from where the dove flew in search of dry land. The ark was a refuge and a

---

[9] Heaney worked on versions of 'the well-known Florentine Catholic' from early in his career, and quoted from Dante as the epigraph to 'The Strand at Lough Beg', for example. There is an interesting line to follow from Dante's marsh to Virgil's riverbank. To Michael Longley, 24 May 1978, *LSH*.

[10] Donald Davie (1922–1995) was an English poet and critic, and a correspondent of Heaney who addressed the Irish poet in his 'Summer Lightning'. To Donald Davie, 17 August 1980, *LSH*.

[11] 'The Flight Path', *SL*.

sanctuary, and suggestive of some wider disturbance beyond, which is in keeping with Heaney's general descriptions of rural Derry before the Troubles, beautiful, if ill at ease. The comparison of the paper boat to a pegged tent is less evident, but is a nod towards a passage in James Joyce's *A Portrait of the Artist as a Young Man* when Stephen attends his school performance. This is the first time the young Dedalus feels the force of lift, the theatre teetering before him as he begins to see the world around him as vision, not reality.[12] The moment is fleeting and subtle. Heaney's attention to it suggests something of his own qualities as a reader, finding significance in oblique moments of transformation. It also suggests Heaney's larger debt to Joyce, even as the speaker sails by it, the paper boat soon soggy in water, sunk.

The second part of the sequence returns to the imagery of flight, and expands it into an elevation and a leaving. Heaney builds the poem like a pattern through its parts, each worked into a wider and a deeper form than he began with. The mysteries of the forge were among his first fascinations, and even now, decades later, the poems are handled like a shape made from base materials, which in the poem's case are memory and experience. There is a kind of mathematical measurement in this work too, which is surprising as so many of the poems proceed from the emotions. Calibrating feeling with form is another way to describe how Heaney calculates his bearings, the artistic rendering of which is the substance of the poems. In the second part of 'The Flight Path' the speaker imagines himself at the day's end, looking up:

> Equal and opposite, the part that lifts
> Into those *full-starred heavens that winter sees*
> When I stand in Wicklow under the flight path
> Of a late jet out of Dublin, its risen light

---

[12] This is in turn one of the greatest passages from all of Joyce. Stephen 'passed out of the schoolhouse and halted under the shed that flanked the garden. From the theatre opposite came the muffled noise of the audience and sudden brazen clashes of the soldiers' band. The light spread upwards from the glass roof making the theatre seem a festive ark, anchored among the hulks of houses, her frail cables of lanterns looping her to her moorings...His unrest issued from him like a wave of sound: and on the tide of flowing music the ark was journeying, trailing her cables of lanterns in her wake.' James Joyce, *A Portrait of the Artist as a Young Man*.

>   Winking ahead of what it hauls away:
>   Heavy engine noise and its abatement
>   Widening far back down, a wake through starlight.[13]

The lines are littered with images of death and resurrection, 'late', 'risen', and 'wake' three signs of Heaney's mortal thought. These correspond with Heaney's quotation from Thomas Hardy's 'Afterwards', a poem in which Hardy imagined how people might remember him after his death. Hardy was a famous novelist and a poet who had a significant influence on Heaney's art.[14] Tara Christie has written compellingly of Heaney's long awareness of Hardy's sense of language and place, and noticed the edition of the 'Collected Hardy' beside the 'Collected Yeats'[15] in 'The Bookcase'. Hardy's 'Afterwards' has little concern for its literary posterity. Instead, it asks about the inner life and how little it registers in our collective consciousness, Hardy drawing himself as a quiet watcher of the twilight, attentive to nature's small moments. Heaney had worn similar vestment before, and Wicklow was long the province where nature met the night, his speaker listening as the 'sycamore speaks in sycamore from darkness.'[16] His citation of Hardy in 'The Flight Path' is from the fourth and penultimate verse of 'Afterwards', which asks:

>   If, when hearing that I have been stilled at last, they stand at
>   the door,
>   Watching the full-starred heavens that winter sees,
>   Will this thought rise on those who will meet my face no more,
>   'He was one who had an eye for such mysteries'?

---

[13] 'The Flight Path', *SL*.
[14] Thomas Hardy (1840–1928), English novelist and poet, was a long-standing influence on Heaney, who lectured on him at Harvard, selected his poems for *The Rattle Bag*, the anthology Heaney edited with Ted Hughes, and quoted from him in correspondence, calling Hardy a 'dreamforce' in a letter to Jane Feaver, 29 June 2007, *LSH*.
[15] 'The Bookcase', *EL*.
[16] 'The Flight Path', *SL*. There may be a ghost of John Berryman's 'Dream Song 1' in this sycamore song; Heaney was certainly familiar with the American poet, who Heaney had in mind as late as 2009 in a letter to Greg Delanty, *LSH*.

Beyond what Hardy's poem means, the music of the line that Heaney quotes sings against the weight of the moment in his poem, the abatement and the hauling away. 'Afterwards' is a citation and a counterpoint, a line of Hardy's in Heaney's chorus, whose other voices are the trees and the jet, the stars and the 'stay-at-homes'[17] still silent. Heaney's poetry has this quality of modulated sound, pockets of quietude beside images of bustle and movement. It gives the work a watchfulness that is often on the verge of melancholy, which is medicated by movement, flight a leaving and a necessity. Heaney does not self-reflect on these moments, which are the substance of the poems, but lightens the lines, hiding in company as the third section of 'The Flight Path' begins:

> Up and away. The buzz from duty free.
> Black velvet. Bourbon. Love letters on high.
> The spacewalk of Manhattan. The re-entry.[18]

For all that human nature is slow to change, our histories pass quickly, and this poem of carefree air travel is from an age ago, before the planet burned in summer wildfire. Heaney had a deep relationship with American writers and institutions, and visited many over the decades. His first sustained experience of America was his appointment at Berkeley. The incentive was initially financial as the move from Belfast to Wicklow and then Sandymount in the seaside suburbs of Dublin invited precarity, an unwelcome condition with three children soon arriving. Berkeley offered a balance between paid work for one semester and free time the rest of the year, although even that commitment began to feel too much as Heaney was pulled one way and another by public lectures, readings, radio programmes, and a stream of correspondence that might have driven another to become a recluse. He was first there in the early seventies, with flower power still in bloom, and he reported home on the sights of San Francisco with a certain wry amusement, however much he enjoyed the occasional distraction of visitors, such as

---

[17] Ibid.   [18] Ibid.

when the Chieftains came to visit him, sunbathing their white bellies in the garden over glasses of whiskey.[19]

The travel and time eventually told and Heaney finished with Berkeley, refusing posts at other American universities, including Princeton, before he accepted a position at Harvard, which again allowed him visit Cambridge for a semester and be free for the rest of the year. That freedom was curtailed by its own obligations as students and colleagues visited, wrote, and asked for insight and advice. To some degree Heaney was victim of his own gift for sociability, which he shared with an equanimity that never deserted him, no matter how famous he became. Harvard was critical to Heaney for two major reasons, beyond the financial. It connected him with a network of writers and critics who sustained and re-energized him, especially at times when the same community in Ireland could be claustrophobic. It also confirmed his entry to a metropolitan circuit that extended to his subsequent election as the Oxford Professor of Poetry, all of which was confirmed by his career-long publication by Faber, that most establishment of houses. At Harvard, Heaney thrived in the friendship of a broad community of intellectuals and artists. Prime among them were the poet Czeslaw Milosz, the critic Helen Vendler, and the translator and classicist Robert Fitzgerald. Heaney had read Milosz's work for years before he met him, and was in Harvard as an audience member for Milosz's Charles Eliot Norton lectures in 1982. The two met for the first time in the summer of the following year in California. Heaney heard many echoes of Irish experience in the Polish and returned to the comparison on many occasions in his poetry. He also met and maintained friendships with several other Polish poets and translators in Cambridge around Milosz's circle.

Vendler had been an acute reader of Heaney's work for years before she met him, and was one of the key figures in his Harvard appointment. She was a famous, and formalist, close reader of modern American poetry and one of the first to write a book length study of Heaney's poetry. Vendler had a laser intellect and an eye for fine detail.

---

[19] He wrote to his old friend David Hammond that 'the only bit of crack I've had as been the visit of the Chieftains to SF last week...We ended up here in the afternoon and it was a pleasure to see them stripping down to their white farmer's bellies and facing into the bourbon on the rocks'. To David Hammond, 13 May 1976, *LSH*.

She was also a kind and encouraging advocate, and Heaney appreciated deeply her perspective.[20] Fitzgerald was famous for his translations of the *Iliad*, the *Odyssey*, and the *Aeneid*. Heaney met him near the end of his life and associated him with bringing the ancient world to modern speech, a question of form and intonation that can become a major obstacle for any poet who wishes to bring the far past to the present (another Irish analogy for this being Ciaran Carson's difficulty translating Dante until he heard a line as if it was shaped by traditional music). The three together give a sense of the hidden power of a university, which is to make its own little world of the global influences it gathers. Heaney was deeply enriched by this, even as he grumbled while he was there about how little he wrote creatively while thinking about lectures and classes.

On top of all this was a short-term travel schedule of readings and talks, supplemented later by a steady flow of commencement and graduation speeches. Harvard is on the fringe of one of America's deepest Irish communities, which radiates out into a network of community groups, colleges, and towns, each of which has provided an audience and a home for visiting Irish writers and scholars for decades. The popular image of Irish emigration focuses on that north-east quadrant, but its history goes deeper and wider, particularly in the south, where Heaney visited frequently, becoming friends with Ronald Schuchard and Rand Brandes among many others.[21] Schuchard was a long-time professor at Emory University, which thanks to its then Joycean president William Chase, and the financial endowment of the Coca-Cola powered Woodruff foundation, later acquired a generation of Irish literary manuscripts for its special collections libraries, a good portion of Heaney's among them. Heaney was taken with Schuchard's learning and his sociability, two qualities both shared. Like Ciaran Carson he had a familiar feeling for the region, Carson driving through one

---

[20] Helen Vendler (1933–2024) was latterly the A. Kingsley Porter University Professor at Harvard. She was a friend and advocate of Heaney, as well as being a great scholar of Yeats.

[21] Ronald Schuhard was a distinguished member of the English department at Emory University for many years, and is a fine critic of Heaney, Eliot, and Yeats. Rand Brandes was a bibliographer of Heaney and a long-time member of the English department at Lenoir-Rhyne University.

summer evening listening to evangelical radio thinking how much the stress and cadence reminded him of home.

As Heaney's letters show, these literary visits were social occasions that took their personal toll, no matter how he may have enjoyed them. It could all catch up in overwork and exhaustion, neither of which Heaney ever used as an excuse to avoid commitment. Still he went on, listening at last as he got older to his family's requests that he take it easier. Even then the changes brought by age and travel could catch him out, as when he near fell at a graduation ceremony in Scotland, an attentive friend catching him under the arm before he did himself real damage.[22] The poems are more likely to catch the lightheadedness of drink and jet lag than they are these stumbles, elevations that give the poems altitude even after the poet lands on the other side. Heaney's spaced walk opens 'Flight Path' as a portal to Heaney's other poems, which ghost behind this section. Hardy's 'Afterwards' had imagined his friends 'standing at the door' to remember him, an idea that Heaney adapts to remember poems of his that tacked between those twin correspondences, life and memory, death and afterlife. Heaney's 'Remembering Malibu', 'Westering', and his long-standing fascination with the figure of Sweeney are all the shadow architecture of this third section. 'Remembering Malibu' was Heaney's tribute to Brian Moore, and it figures glancingly in 'The Flight Path', the disquiets of Heaney's earlier work abroad now washed away with 'deck-tables and champagne',[23] the seagull's hard stare the only reminder of troubles elsewhere. 'Remembering Malibu' was a poem as much as about Ireland as America in its reconsideration of the land- and seascape that Heaney thought he knew before he left it, just as 'The Flight Path' jumps back to Glanmore for three lines before it takes off again,

> *Jet-sitting next. Across and across and across.*
> *Westering, eastering, the jumbo a school bus,*
> *'The Yard' a cross between the farm and campus,*

---

[22] The incident is recorded in Heaney's letter to Patrick Crotty, 11 May 2011, *LSH*.
[23] 'The Flight Path', *SL*.

> *A holding pattern and a tautening purchase—*
> *Sweeney astray in home truths out of Horace:*
> *Skies change, not cares, for those who cross the seas.*[24]

Heaney's overuse of repetition is a feature of the later poems. It gives the verses a pausing rhythm that is somewhere between hesitancy and translation, the stringing together of descriptive words a chain that leads back to his fascination with Anglo-Saxon. Now he summons 'Westering' as the link between Ireland, America, and the night sky, the gravity of that poem stilling 'The Flight Path', the poet caught in a holding pattern. The earlier melancholy returns in the warning from Horace's epistles, which is that no matter how far we travel, what we carry we bring with us. The counterpoint for this is Sweeney, another of Heaney's dream figures, and a story and an idea that Heaney returned to for decades. Sweeney fled his kingship after being cursed by a saint and banished in the form of a bird. His exile resonated with Heaney, who was caught often between the close territories of the north and its troubles, and the world that opened beyond Glanmore. Heaney crossed these fraught mental landscapes with a guilt that diminished after the violence faded. 'The Flight Path' is a poem of transitions and the correspondence between Sweeney and Horace prepares the ground for an unresolved confrontation from decades previous. On the train from Dublin to Belfast after a night flight from New York the poet was challenged by a man he had known since childhood and who Heaney knew to be a republican.

> 'When, for fuck's sake, are you going to write
> Something for us?' 'If I do write something,
> Whatever it is, I'll be writing for myself.'
> And that was that. Or words to that effect.[25]

The cagey drama of the exchange masks another aspect to the poem, which is its fellow-feeling with other poems of the borderlands, such as Paul Muldoon's 'Unapproved Road', in which Muldoon describes the

---

[24] Ibid.   [25] Ibid.

feeling of crossing the border as holding breath underwater. After allusions to Sweeney and Horace, the sequence closes with a summons of Dante and Virgil:

> Out of Long Kesh after his dirty protest
> The red eyes were the eyes of Ciaran Nugent
> Like something out of Dante's scurry hell,
> Drilling their way through the rhymes and images
> Where I too walked behind the righteous Virgil,
> As safe as houses and translating freely:
> *When he had said all this, his eyes rolled*
> *And his teeth, like a dog's teeth clamping round a bone,*
> *Bit into the skull and again took hold.*[26]

There is an earlier version of Heaney here too, the swinging lights of the fake army patrol in 'The Strand at Lough Beg' reflected in the red of Nugent's eyes. Dante too had featured before, giving way to Virgil as Heaney aged and looked for a more sparing guide. The intensity of the poem diminishes with the return north, although the tendency to summon other selves continues in the allusions to policemen, roadblocks, and a sense of spiritual suffering. The close of the poem has some of the best of later Heaney, and the worst (where, for example, does 'bigly' come in?), the poet bending time in words that become vehicles for a presence that is of the substance of the late voice. For example, when the policeman mishears the poet say he is from 'far away' when he is questioned where he comes from, he says that 'far away' is now a place,

> —both where I have been living
> And where I left—a distance still to go
> Like starlight that is light years on the go
> From far away and takes light years arriving.[27]

---

[26] Ibid.   [27] Ibid.

Gone from this is the melancholy of a poem like 'Exposure', when Heaney worried that he might miss a sky-lit portent so gripped was he by the winter ground. Present is the repetition that twists words into new meanings, even as they return. In this formula 'light years' is less an unimaginable distance than a continuing present in which the poet, and the poem, live. The ritual roots of this secular transfiguration are deep in Heaney's mind and go back into the first poems about funerals, school, and retreats. 'The Flight Path' brings these inheritances together as the poem faces in its last direction, south towards the French pilgrim town of Rocamadour, the stone steps up a sunny hill, 'sheer exaltation':[28]

> Eleven in the morning. I made a note:
> 'Rock-lover, loner, sky-sentry, all hail!'
> And somewhere the dove rose. And kept on rising.[29]

Heaney loved the imagery of elevation, his poems moving from the muck and mud to the light and air, mist and rain the symbol of their challenges, the sun a resolution that dips towards twilight as the poems laten. Even then trajectory is not a set progress, and one of the highest compliments Heaney pays another artist is when his own work marks the other as creating a new degree of observation, as he does in 'Wordsworth's Skates'. The English lyric had a deep purchase in Heaney's imagination, as did its landscape, at least as an assembly of words from which to depart. His recognition of this layer of allusion figures as citation in several of the poems, as it did with the reference to Hardy in 'The Flight Path'. In 'Wordsworth's Skates' there is a different exchange, beyond quotation. Instead, Heaney sees Wordsworth as a fellow presence, earthbound and starstruck, the twin blades of his ice skates freed from their display case and out on 'frozen Windermere',[30] as Wordsworth

> flashed from the clutch of earth along its curve
> And left it scored.[31]

[28] Ibid.   [29] Ibid.   [30] 'Wordsworth's Skates', *DC*.   [31] Ibid.

That last word lingers with disquiet, unless it is read musically, as if Wordsworth set the English language in new relation to the elements around it. Similarly sharp words mark another of Heaney's poems, 'A Scuttle for Dorothy Wordsworth', which is a short two-verse lyric that has something of the skating poem's lift, and its cuttingness.[32] In it, the young Dorothy has a toothache 'ablaze',[33] her body stung by the 'jolt and jag'[34] of her frayed nerve endings. Older, she is reduced to a 'flicker',[35] alone. The scuttle poem is one of two that make up the 'Home Fires' sequence, the second of which is 'A Stove Lid for W. H. Auden'. This begins with a moment of equilibrium in a quotation from Auden's 'The Shield of Achilles':[36]

> The mass and majesty of this world, all
> That carries weight and always weighs the same...[37]

The familiar reader might think this a moment of equilibrium, such as Heaney often tried to find. The late truth is different, and darker, as Auden's poem is more about the continuity of violence than its resolution in peace. In Auden the shield is a barren work, the iron image of an abstract world and not that world's organic incarnation. 'The Shield of Achilles' is a study of shortened lives, the man-killing hero the symbol of divine malfunction. Heaney reworks Auden's poem by reducing its human scale. Where in Auden there is a marching army, in Heaney the ranks are reduced to poem and reader, rendered in 'the small compass of a cast-iron stove lid.'[38] The burner is a 'fire-fanged maw' of a 'gnashing bucket',[39] the animal teeth reminiscent of Dante's dogs, images that hang in the background like ghosts. 'The Shield of Achilles' ended with its maker Hephaestos hobbling away, taut-mouthed as if the armourer had

---

[32] Dorothy Wordsworth (1771–1855), poet and author.
[33] 'Home Fires 1: A Scuttle for Dorothy Wordsworth', DC.   [34] Ibid.   [35] Ibid.
[36] W. H Auden (1907–1973) was a poet Heaney frequently read and referred to, including in Heaney's T. S. Eliot lectures at the University of Kent at Canterbury in 1986. Heaney also wrote a poem called 'Audenesque' in memory of Joseph Brodsky and published in EL. Joseph Brodsky (1940–1996) was a poet and essayist, born in Russia, later emigrating to America. He was awarded the Nobel Prize for Literature in 1987.
[37] 'Home Fires 2: A Stove Lid for W. H. Auden', DC.   [38] Ibid.
[39] Ibid.

nothing to say of his work but disapproval. Heaney's poem offers a different view:

> So one more time,
> I tote it, hell-mouth stopper, flat-earth disc,
> And replace it safely. Wherefore rake and rattle,
> Watch sparks die in the ashpan, poke again,
> Think of dark matter in the starlit coalhouse.[40]

This is the flammable poem, art the careful practice of enlightenment by fire, poetry the sifted remains of the burnt. The image softens into something more cosmic in the last lines, Heaney considering the skies as a source of illumination as he did so often. But there is an admission here too that however the poet has built new means of process and observation, the actual matter of art is still as it was, inflammation. The embers of this observation smouldered in Heaney's poetry for a long time too, and are sensible in the remains of a blacksmith's workings, or the engine of a passing train. They are there again in Heaney's admiration for Rainer Maria Rilke, the Austro-German poet whose melancholy sense of a spiritually animated world often leaves the reader wonder what place the human has in it at all.[41] Heaney wrote versions of two Rilke poems in his later collections, one of which speaks directly to the difficulty of illumination. 'After the Fire' describes the moment after a farmhouse has burned down, the son of the house managing his shock by retrieving twisted metal that was the day before a kettle or a pot from the heat. There is no mention of his relatives, but for the fact he is now alone.

> For now that it was gone, it all seemed
> Far stranger: more fantastical than Pharaoh.
> And he was changed: a foreigner among them.[42]

The carbon aftermath of these fiery poems is Heaney's 'dark matter',[43] the ash of histories that have been consumed, but not lost. The poet had

---

[40] Ibid.
[41] Rainer Maria Rilke (1875–1926) was an Austro-German poet whose 'deep inner...dark' Heaney recognized. Letter to Dennis O'Driscoll, 29 March 2005, *LSH*.
[42] 'Rilke: After the Fire', *DC*.   [43] Ibid.

hoped for more substantial survival years before ('If I could come on meteorite!'[44]). Later he settled for the visibility of traces, from which he made poetic forms. Heaney's use of dust and ash is an important metaphor to understand these imagined relationships as it is both material and molecular, lightly worn and unavoidable, a settlement, as it were, of the poet's making.

Another version of this is 'The Border Campaign', which Heaney dedicated to Nadine Gordimer. Gordimer was a fellow Nobel Prize winner who wrote of her native South Africa during and after apartheid.[45] 'The Border Campaign' is a poem about childhood memory that also cites another of Heaney's abiding influences, in *Beowulf*. This gives a strange quality to the poem, part north, part south, part contemporary, part historic, barbarity and resistance the binding themes:

> Soot-streaks down the courthouse wall, a hole
> Smashed in the roof, the rafters in the rain
> Still smouldering:
>   when I heard the word 'attack'
> In St Columb's College in nineteen fifty-six
> It left me winded, left nothing between me
> And the sky that moved beyond my boarder's dormer[46]

Heaney's elemental sense of himself grew as he aged, those moments where he imagined himself in the wind and light related to his own experience of time. This is connected too to whatever spiritual sense the poetry retains beyond the community rituals of established religion. Considered like this, Heaney's compulsion to draw his life experience through proximity to the fantastical horror of Grendel makes his interest in *Beowulf* a mediumship between the far north and the near, in time and place. It begins to explain the flood of Anglo-Saxon mannerisms in the later poetry, which are a sign of how deeply Heaney tried to put a

---

[44] 'Exposure', *N*.
[45] Nadine Gordimer (1923–2014) was a South African writer and activist who received the Nobel Prize for Literature in 1991. Heaney met her at the International Writers' Festival in Dublin in 1993. To Bernard and Jane MacCabe, 9 October 1993, *LSH*.
[46] 'The Border Campaign', *EL*.

pattern on the embodiment of difficult memory. At times this becomes a distraction, the poems squirming into alliterative shapes that mimic the kenning's compound forms. At others, these miniature, internal sequences create forms of perception that are diffuse and transcendent, the poems environments, not statements. 'The Border Campaign' approaches this condition as the late Heaney imagines his younger self in the first approach to this realization, reflecting that

>   All that was written
>   And to come I was a part of then...[47]

Unusually, it ends with a fragment of direct quotation from what would become Heaney's later version of the whole of *Beowulf*:

>   *Every nail and claw-spike, every spur*
>   *And hackle and hand-barb on that heathen brute*
>   *Was like a steel prong in the morning dew.*[48]

The closing words are a hymn to water as the bridging element between pain and persistence, the 'morning dew' a balm of liquid and light that together can banish Grendel's harsh domain. But where *Beowulf* is a study in the persistence of human society, 'The Border Campaign' suggests another dimension to Heaney's understanding of the poem, which is its solitariness. Beowulf is a figure of song more than he is commander of a cohort, a hero alone in lands far from home. Heaney's poetic versions of himself are similarly in company but detached. In Heaney's poem for Gordimer the conditions for this alienation are social and historical, the rumblings of the northern Troubles echoing in apartheid South Africa.

This global north resonated closer to home too, and was connected by another earlier text, in this case Heaney's abiding fascination with the legend of Sweeney, and through it the islands of Scotland. The poet's interest in Sweeney can be overshadowed by his late obsession with

---

[47] Ibid.   [48] Ibid.

Beowulf, but the early Irish text aligned with Heaney's general sense of flight, experience, and return. Sweeney suffered terribly, crippled by a curse that cost him his sovereignty and his family. His bird flight allowed Heaney in turn to draw the land- and seascapes of the north in new dimensions from above, Sweeney flitting from branch to rock in all weathers. His motion opened a north beyond the shores of Ireland, his territory bordered by the sea around Ailsa Craig, an island in the Firth of Clyde. This watery archipelago joined Ireland to Scotland in a string of island attachments that were unmoored from the weight of Britishness. Louis MacNeice had explored the way a generation before, but found no way through but leaving, the hard declensions of the north too unforgiving for an imagination that liked to wander.

Heaney drew the map differently, and with it the experience of engaging with Scottish writers who, like himself, worked in an English language hammered and heated into new forms. Poems in the later books make a sequence of studies of Hugh MacDiarmid, Norman MacCaig, Sorley MacLean, and George Mackay Brown, the male company of which pulls together Heaney's impressions of their collective place.[49] The intersection between gender, language, and place is legible in several of Heaney's poems about Ireland, and especially Derry. The bog poems too associate the premodern, prehistoric landscapes of northern Europe with a female energy whose dues are paid in different form than those of a later, Anglocentric, colonialism. Heaney heard echoes of this old world in a poem like Sorley MacLean's 'Hallaig', which Heaney made a version of from one of Ian Crichton Smith's translations, which he first discovered in the seventies.[50] MacLean was from the island of Raasay and his poem is its imaginary repopulation. As with Ireland, migration and clearance meant psychological and linguistic

---

[49] Hugh MacDiarmid was the pseudonym of C. M. Grieve (1892–1978), a Scottish poet and visionary; Norman MacCaig (1910–1996) was a Scottish poet and teacher; Sorley MacLean (1911–1996) was a Gaelic poet of the western isles, born on Raasay; George Mackay Brown (1921–1996) was a Scottish author and broadcaster. Heaney had recorded a radio interview with MacDiarmid as early as 1974, on Patrick Kavanagh's theme of the parish and the universe, a concern Heaney recognized in his Scottish neighbours. To John Montague, 23 January 1974, *LSH*.

[50] Iain Crichton Smith (1928–1998) was a Scottish poet, journalist and author whose work Heaney admired, as described in a letter to Barrie Cooke, 19 March 1976, *LSH*.

distress. MacLean made this into a poetry of vision, which had the strength not to turn to nightmare. That 'vivid speechless air'[51] connected with Heaney on a frequency that carried over the Irish Sea to the western isles and up north to Orkney and then to Shetland. The axis around which this all turned was MacDiarmid, who Heaney summons in 'An Invocation'. This is a poem that is somewhere between an order and a tribute, and which begins with one of those lines of Heaney's that stays in the mind for its music as much as its meaning.

> Incline to me, MacDiarmid, out of Shetland,
> Stone-eyed from stone-gazing, sobered up
> And thrawn.[52]

Even this short sentence says so much of Heaney's later style, the braid of repetition and dialect giving the poem a twisted energy, ready to unspring in lines that veer off into the memory of MacDiarmid as he could be, drunk and contrary. The MacDiarmid Heaney remembers is a particular one, fled as far north as he could and still be in Scotland. MacDiarmid is an avatar of Sweeney, a 'gatekeeper/ Of the open gates behind the brows of birds',[53] his dispersed sentience a form of afterlife in the poetry, 'Beyond the stony limits, writing-mad.'[54] The thought occurs here of the tomb, and Heaney's poem is its own rolling away of the block he had sent between his younger self and MacDiarmid, who the earlier Heaney had taken partly for a fool. Now Heaney registers experience as the capacity to set the mind in correspondence with the real, as MacDiarmid sometimes managed to do,

> Your big pale forehead in the window glass
> Like the earth's curve on the sea's curve to the north.[55]

The poem doubts whether MacDiarmid will answer its call, an admission after all that rhetoric has little purchase over the wild, and the visionary.

---

[51] *Hallaig* by Somhairle MacGill-Eain. Translated by Seamus Heaney (Urras Shomhairle/ The Sorley MacLean Trust: Dunblane, 2002).
[52] 'An Invocation', *SL*.   [53] Ibid.   [54] Ibid.   [55] Ibid.

In this sense the poem flattens out in its closing stanza, resorting to formula instead of observation. Resolute is the idea that poetry itself is

> A function of its time and place
> And sometimes of our own.[56]

This is the heart of the matter, and puts simply the idea that art has its province, with poetry its portal. Macdiarmid is at one extremity of this mental territory, MacCaig and the rest gathered closer in, the rocky outpost of the Shetlands giving way to Orkney and the western isles. The sequence of short lyrics that compose 'Would They Had Stay'd' has its foundation in depopulation and language loss, Scottish Gaelic a tattoo on Heaney's English, the echoes of colonization sounding through the poem's landscapes. This work is about attention and scale, the world measured in the miniature structures of leaf and stem, 'meadow hay' and 'meadow-sweet'.[57] Deeper again are the imprints of the past on these lonely places, Norman MacCaig imagined as 'fawn' and 'gallowglass',[58] the vulnerable and the rebel hidden in a stilled land. Other Scottish poets are caught too, mirages in the high country, sorrowful and marked by war. George Mackay Brown is different, the whole worked to a final figure in which place and the imagination take the tangible form of poetry.

> What George Mackay Brown saw was a drinking deer
> That glittered by the water. The human soul
> In mosaic. Wet celandine and ivy.
> Allegory hard as a figured shield
> Smithied in Orkney for Christ's sake and Crusades,
> Polished until its undersurface surfaced
> Like peat smoke mulling through Byzantium.[59]

As so often with these poems, there is a veiled figure in the background, legible in language by implication. The echo of Yeats sounds through Heaney's Scottish poem in the metal-worked form of the shield, the

---

[56] Ibid.   [57] 'Would they had Stay'd', *EL*.   [58] Ibid.   [59] Ibid.

inescapable outward form of the object unwritten by its polished interior. The journey in Yeats's 'Sailing to Byzantium' was from the Irish Sea to the Bosphorus, from poetry to sculptured form. Heaney's poem is similarly about transfiguration, which turns to dispersal, the peat smoke in Byzantium a layer of time and sensation that is spectral in its suggestion, an image of evening time in the depths of history. This is in keeping with the late sense of Heaney's art, not least since so many of his bearings were past or passing. Like Virgil in the countryside, Yeats was a guide in this late panorama, the shifting pieces of life's mosaic given one possible shape by the earlier poet's metaphorical world. The resource is there elsewhere in Heaney's dedicatory poems, as in his memorial for Milosz, the loss of whose influence he lamented in 'Saw Music (Out of this World)', the title of which referred to Milosz's poem, 'The World'.

Heaney's poem is in three parts, the first two of which play with his memories of mass and pilgrimage as a child, which leads him to think about the words we use to describe the indescribable. Again, the poem returns to Heaney's late bearing, which is that moment between earth and air, when art lifts off and becomes something more than its elements. What is drawn elsewhere as the experience of flight is caught more thickly now as grief and transcendence, Heaney's mediators extending to Yeats and the painter Barrie Cooke.

> Barrie Cooke has begun to paint 'godbeams',
> Vents of brightness that make the light of heaven
> Look like stretched sheets of fluted silk or rayon
> In an old-style draper's window. Airslides, scrims
>
> And scumble. Columnar sift. But his actual palette
> Is ever sludge and smudge, as if a shower
> Made puddles on the spirit's winnowing floor.[60]

Mosaic is too hard a word, and too fragmentary, to catch the style of these last poems, but it gets towards Heaney's partial, recycling style, the light of other poems like Heaney's for his aunt and for Bruegel like an

---

[60] 'Out of this World 3: Saw Music', *DC*.

invisible knot that ties all together. The late poems are anthology and innovation, the form a half-rhyme with what came before. Changed is the tone, and the tendency to stop a line with internal phrases that break the rhythm with short spaces between each full stop. Grammar is a brook in these poems, a gathering of the words' flow in spaces that compress their energy in momentary stays of attention. The two stanzas above show one example of this technique, the first three lines running free into the slower bridge of the images that join the two verses before the poem takes off again, with reservation, 'But' giving way to 'as if'. The doubt that any art can capture the unreality of being prepares a question that Heaney often asks, which is why poetry matters? Cooke's art gives one answer by analogy, his light shafts an interruption of the everyday in grand, unexpected style. Milosz had his answer too, as Heaney shares:

> 'The art of oil painting—
> Daubs fixed on canvas—is a paltry thing
> Compared with what cries out to be expressed,'
>
> The poet said, who lies this god-beamed day
> Coffined in Krakow, as out of this world now
> As the untranscendent music of the saw
> He might have heard in Vilnius or Warsaw
>
> And would not have renounced, however paltry.[61]

Much as things changed in Heaney's later life and writing, constant was the sense of qualification, even, or especially, in memorial. There are five figures in these closing lines: Heaney, Milosz, Cooke, the saw player, and Yeats. Together they form a ghostly chorus, the sound of which is the wobbling saw, an unmusical instrument, an object made for something else. Seeing the mutability of things is one role for an empathetic poetry, which hears humanity in discord. This much brings Heaney and Milosz together. By analogy, it extends to Cooke, the troubled weather of his paintings shot through with brighter light. Yeats, however, is more difficult, and deeper since the Yeats poem Heaney is referring to is one

---

[61] Ibid.

long held in his own mind. Milosz's suggestion that art cannot capture the complexity of life is adjusted by Heaney's citation of Yeats's 'paltry'. Already 'Sailing to Byzantium' had given Heaney the title for 'Singing School', Heaney's poem about St. Columb's. Now it gives 'Saw Music' part of its attitude to old age, as in Yeats, when

> An aged man is but a paltry thing,
> A tattered coat upon a stick, unless
> Soul clap its hands and sing, and louder sing
> For every tatter in its mortal dress[62]

In Heaney, the body has more elemental form, and soulful. The two are integrated like the mud and light of Cooke's palette, and to separate them is to lose something both of an attitude to life, and to poetry. Bringing Milosz into this equation shows how Heaney remembered his friend, even as he changed him. In the end this is how elegies work, the voiceless dead given different life by those who speak for them. Here it shows something of Heaney's attitude to other artists throughout his writing life, an attitude generous and conditional, the situation weighing on the subject. Changed in this memorial for Milosz is Heaney's sense of scale. His poem is consciously European, and tied through Milosz and Yeats to the great destructions of the twentieth century. In repair is a song to the ill-fitting and the everyday, through which registers whatever passes for the divine, or the consoling. This opacity thins in the late poems to a transparency, luminous and enlightening. Sometimes, it is true, the lines falter, as they do at the very end of 'Saw Music'. Sometimes, too, the light of elsewhere casts this world in shade, Heaney a ghost before he left it.

In this, Heaney followed the example of Milosz one last time. After Milosz died, Heaney said the two poets shared a common attitude in face of mortality, of gratitude. The model Heaney chose to illustrate this negotiation between life and death was his version of lines from Sophocles's play, *Oedipus at Colonus*. The Greek drama has its Irish provenance in that Yeats had written a version of the play for an Abbey

---

[62] W. B. Yeats, 'Sailing to Byzantium'.

Theatre production in 1927. Heaney focused on its later lines, which describe Oedipus's final journey into the underworld. He is accompanied there by Theseus, king of Athens, whose reward for admitting Oedipus, blinded and reviled, to Colonus was the secret knowledge of the place between the living earth and after. So long as that secret was known and guarded by the king of Athens, that king and his city would be safe from all turmoil and threat. Heaney called his poem 'What Passed at Colonus' and published it in the *New York Review of Books* in October 2004 in memory of Milosz. It begins with an air of the hedge school, warmed by Attic light, 'his company and voice...like high tidings in the summer trees'.[63] The occasion, however, is mortal, and Oedipus turns and leaves towards a stream running underground.

> And there he stood, studying what next,
> Between a stone cairn and a marble plaque
> To the dead of our late wars.
> Other wars and words were in my mind,
> Another last look taken upon earth—
> *Roads shining after rain*
> *Like uphill rivers*—so that I all but
> Wept for his loneliness.[64]

Sophocles's *Oedipus* is a play framed by conflict. Theseus's welcome to Odysseus invites war between Athens and Thebes, and the death of Oedipus's two warring sons. The lines in italics are from a different conflict and a later, and discovered in the pockets of Edward Thomas after he was killed at Arras in April 1917. Death is an undoing of the bearings, even as it sets a new path. Heaney's evocation of the underworld as a delta of the undead is confirmed in the echo of voices that carry from the opening, a 'waterfall of sound' that gives way to the 'brilliant light'[65] that signals Oedipus's last journey. Then there is quiet:

---

[63] 'What Passed at Colonus', *New York Review of Books*, 7 October 2004.
[64] Ibid.   [65] Ibid.

> No god had galloped
> His thunder chariot, no hurricane
> Had swept the hill. Call me mad, if you like,
> Or gullible, but that man surely went
> In step with a guide he trusted down to where
> Light has gone out but the door stands open.[66]

For all the many traditions of the afterlife that Heaney encountered in his art, his approach to mortality remained the same. From Sophocles to Edward Thomas and then on to Milosz, and finally to himself, Heaney looked through the door into the dark, fully expecting illumination. If light came and went, poetry was an art of the shades, ghosts ungoverned by place and time. Heaney had experimented with these after images for years. Death was a familiar from his early life due to accident and circumstance, just as the rhythm of his childhood was set by the seasonal cycles of his community. These dispositions flowed into a sensual awareness of the landscape, and a widening circle of language and friendship. His greatest tribute to Milosz was to gather these practices in a poem whose substance is the elements of Heaney's late art, of light and water. Liberated from the demands of the here and now, Heaney's Oedipus is, like his Thomas and Milosz, the outline of a near future in which Heaney too would join the company of ghosts.

Late Heaney. Nicholas Allen, Oxford University Press. © Nicholas Allen 2026.
DOI: 10.1093/9780198985419.003.0003

---

[66] Ibid.

4
Ghosts

So much of Irish literature is haunted that it can be hard to see one ghost from another. The source of these sensory disruptions has been identified in many places. Religion is a factor, as is folk belief, and history, each of which has its own ways of narrating deep social fissures. Added to this for the artist is a willingness to accept the boundaries of what is known, and what is not, and leave a door open between.[1] This could admit all kinds of presences, welcome or otherwise, the murdered still clad in the injustice of their last moments. Heaney persisted nonetheless, his attention to the dead as various as the lives they had lived. With this realization came an exploration of the landscapes that ghosts might inhabit. In part this may relate to Heaney's own experience of childhood trauma. His first home was also where his younger brother died in an accident, a disturbance registered in 'Mid-Term Break'. It is a given of modern literature that ghosts equate with hauntings, fogs, and dark nights. There are certainly plenty of those all through Heaney's writing. He had, however, never been afraid of the dark, and as he aged, the panorama of the future became unexpectedly brighter. His ghosts did not disappear in this light but took on different forms, of companionship and not rebuke. The whole had the effect of drawing a once familiar countryside in the lines of Virgil, Derry an Elysium that once was a charnel house.

Even this late bloom had its literary roots deep in Heaney's writing. The familiarity of Mossbawn proceeded from the presence in fields and ditches of the past generations, a condition that Heaney called prehistorical, which is another way of saying there was less boundary between the here and now and the here and then as might obtain in other places. Settlement, of course, is at the heart of that community's

---

[1] Or what Heaney described in a letter to Ted Hughes as the going 'round about the dark of the mind's moon' to 'come back beyond...as poetry'. To Ted Hughes, 14 December 1997, *LSH*.

determination to be fixed where it stood, Bellaghy one square in a patchwork of seventeenth-century plantation, the outlines of which are still visible, colour coded by one town or another's attachment to royalty or republic. The ghosts of this centuries-old conflict are the repertory theatre of Heaney's poetry, their occasional voices a chorus on the fringes of the natural world that was for him the domain of love and family. Beyond this was the prospect of violence, the red lights of paramilitary check-points like 'dogs' eyes in a demon pack'.[2] In this political geography ghosts were symbols of injustice. They outlined the failure of a state to protect them while living, without having to declare the details of their own lived thoughts or experience. They were mediums, in their way, for the frustrations Heaney felt with the lockstep tension of the north, a place so drenched in repetitive politics it seemed the horizon might never brighten. It did, slowly and uncertainly, and with it Heaney's poetry registered a change too. He had long left the north by the time peace came in the mid-nineties, but the place never left him, and he visited regularly to see family and friends. The townlands of his early life had remained a refuge from his writing life, even if the Nobel brought more readers in search of the sites of the poems, and the people in them.

The end of the Troubles, if they can be said even now to be over, coincided with Heaney's rise to the height of his fame as a writer, and with an awareness of his own beginning to age. At the same time his reading changed too, beginning to move from the blood feuds of *Beowulf* to the more varied districts of the *Aeneid*. This last was a bridge from brutality to enlightenment, which was a transition not without its irony given Virgil's imperial provenance, as Heaney knew. He took what was resonant for him from the Latin poem, which was in Heaney's case the construction of death as a life after life, the underworld an image of what remained after the labour of life had passed. It is suggestive to think of Heaney's understanding of Book Six of the *Aeneid* as informed by his own sense of the Derry landscape, divided as both are into appropriate districts. Heaney had wondered about the fitness of poetry to travel these distances, from the inner territory of the lyric to the outer

[2] 'The Strand at Lough Beg', *FW*.

boundaries of war and suffering. His versions of Virgil's *Eclogues* are little trial-pieces in this process, which was carried out on a larger scale in *The Cure at Troy*. This was Heaney's version of Sophocles's *Philoctetes*, which dramatized the rescue of the abandoned warrior whose bow alone will secure the Argives' victory. In Heaney's hands it becomes a play about the end of violence and the resilience of the imagination in the face of bitter feud. It resonated to the degree that its chorus became a kind of proxy for the peace process itself and was often quoted:

> History says, don't hope
> On this side of the grave.
> But then, once in a lifetime
> The longed-for tidal wave
> Of justice can rise up,
> And hope and history rhyme.[3]

Less obvious then was the wider shift in Heaney's writing these lines invited. The political circumstances of the play are well documented, even if the Good Friday Agreement was not at the time the predestined peace agreement it has seemed to appear in retrospect.[4] The rare outbreak of hope prompted Heaney to remind his audience that all such fundamental change proceeded from a capacity to see the ghost of the future in the turmoil of the present:

> If there's fire on the mountain
> Or lightning and storm
> And a god speaks from the sky
>
> That means someone is hearing
> The outcry and the birth-cry
> of new life at its term.[5]

---

[3] *CAT*.
[4] One of the challenges of reading this period is the degree to which the sequence of historical events that led to a cessation, mostly, of political violence, does not necessarily correspond with the lived experiences of individuals and communities traumatized by decades of unrest. The chorus gives hope a voice, but the under bass remains.
[5] *CAT*.

In the years following Heaney wrote in the realization that this new birth might be long past his own lifetime, a deferral that came with a self-awareness that he worked slowly into a liberation. The late poetry is a porous art, ghostly in its forms and imagery, its apparitions visible in the sun and evening light. It is a theatre of presences, which can give the places and people he writes about the quality of a watercolour, itself in keeping with his lifelong interest in the visual arts. Writing to Barrie Cooke, Heaney remembered Constable's line that the puddles and clouds of his youth had made him into a painter.[6] Heaney felt similarly, and his sense of reflection only grew with time, some of his very last poems written under 'the dome of the sky'.[7] The poet, and the people he writes about, the earth and water, trees, rivers, fish and cattle, are all presences in the poetry, as if lit by electric light. The alabaster effect makes the solid less so and introduces the idea that ghostliness might not mean a haunting but a heightened awareness, which is another way for art to find a freedom from history without denying the legitimacy of either. It might explain too why so many readers with such different experiences than Heaney find resonance in his work, the animation of a luminous world the operation of an imagination whose language is empathy and dream.

Looking back, much of Heaney's poetry was concerned with the dead, and where to put them in the grand scheme of life. The earliest work is shadowed by family loss, which shades in the mid-period into political violence, the landscapes of the north outlined in hellish light. The later poetry is different, even as the end comes nearer. Fired by a spectral light that radiates through the rural Derry of Heaney's memory, these poems are part of this world, and part of another, the bridge between Heaney's absorption in John Donne, Virgil, and the merger of his memories with an awareness of the changes that his stroke caused. The most remarkable transition in these late poems is that of Heaney himself. He becomes his own ghost, the poet using his art to imagine

---

[6] 'I've always loved that statement that Constable made somewhere about old muddy banks and puddles and sheughs—not his word—having made a painter of him'. To Basil Blackshaw, 14 February 2000, *LSH*. 'Sheugh' is an Ulster-Scots word for a ditch or drain, sometimes used to mark a boundary.
[7] 'The Riverbank Field', *HC*.

himself in dimensions beyond the everyday, his poetry a leave-taking and a testament, all written in love for his family and his chosen ground. Heaney had prepared for this for a long time. He was often alone in his work, and watchful even in company. Age brought a change, as did recognition, Heaney declaring in his Nobel acceptance speech that he had finally found the way to look the world eye to eye, and no longer be bowed by its weight.

It was as if Heaney had washed up on a far shore beyond Lough and sea. There is a compact version of this journey in Heaney's adaptation of Alexander Pushkin's 'Arion', which tells of shipwreck and survival. The subject is a poet who sings to his crew as they row, before the boat founders in a squall.

> The helmsman and the sailors perished.
> Only I, still singing, washed
> Ashore by the long sea-swell, sing on,
> A mystery to my poet self,
> And safe and sound beneath a rock shelf
> Have spread my wet clothes in the sun.[8]

Survival and self-exposure are deep elements of Heaney's poetry, and joy a late arrival. The acceptance of forgetting is new too, tied as it is to the admission that words cannot fix everything, or put reality in livable shape. That Heaney discovered this without surrendering to resignation gives the late work the combined power of free testimony. The poems admit loss and regret as companions to love and contentment, the mingled forms of which take shape in Heaney's elegies for his parents, such as in 'Album', a five-part sequence in memory of his father. Like many of these poems, water is the medium of Heaney's imagination, the scene set of his mother and father moving from the summer countryside of Derry to the seaside, the soundtrack

> A skirl of gulls. A smell of cooking fish.
> Plump dormant silver. Stranded silence. Tears.[9]

[8] 'Arion', *EL*.   [9] 'Album', *HC*.

The echo of the earlier poems of killing unsettles the surface of the picture, as do the tears, which suggest a configuration of the body as water. Then it worked to make whole the desecrated remains of a murder victim. Now it creates a channel between those different passages of the past that are unresolved, because disconnected. The poem is a work in progress towards a gathering, which Heaney works out in its last two parts, beginning, as he always did, with what he might do had he the chance again:

> Were I to have embraced him anywhere
> It would have been on the riverbank.[10]

He did not this time, but in imagining that he might have, he summons one of the key places in his late poetry, the riverbank. The place owes much to Virgil's imaginations of the other world, but Heaney's arrival there is his own doing. The journey is all by water, the poem describing two later times when he did hold his father, once at 'New Ferry' and again

> ...on the landing during his last week,
> Helping him to the bathroom, my right arm
> Taking the webby weight of his underarm.[11]

The house floats here, the landing a haven for boats as much as a space upstairs. The poem's punning quality is of a kind with its fluidity, everything slightly unmoored, and adrift. Sometimes Heaney welcomed this letting go as a kind of freedom, as he does in the beautiful 'A Kite for Aibhín', or even in 'Postscript'. More often, it has a broken quality, the proof of the moment drawn in regret, or missed opportunity. There is a little of this in 'Album''s closing lines,

> Just as a moment back a son's three tries
> At an embrace in Elysium

---

[10] Ibid.   [11] Ibid.

Swam up into my very arms, and in and out
Of the Latin stem itself, the phantom
Verus that has slipped from 'very'.[12]

Hidden in the poem's motions is the slippage between the poet and his father, both as ghosts. Elysium is Virgil's land of the exalted dead, where the citizens who gave great service share the afterlives due their selflessness. The poem is at once a tribute to Heaney's father and a step in the river, a transition that Heaney plays with in other poems in *Human Chain*, to which we will return. The figure of the past as a body of water was long there. The turn now is inward, the boundaries of earth and water giving way to light and shade, the materiality of the past receding before a present that is all too aware of its own short future. In other artists this might invite gloom, or resignation. Heaney manages a different tone in these late poems, the pitch of which is set deep in the work that came before.

All of Heaney's poetry depends on the transformation of complex feeling into workable form. Earlier those forms took shape from what was to hand, and well known. Later they were speculative, and more open to mystery. The religious analogy might be to the act of communion, and certainly the Troubles gave every opportunity for blood and flesh to live again in art. The poet, however, has no divine right, and a sectarian war might give pause to religious feeling in the work. So the ghosts appear in a space between rite and circumstance, the later poems a watercolour of the past, washed with spirits. 'Two Lorries' captures this picture perfectly, written as it is between two memories of Heaney's mother, and of Magherafelt. The prompt for the poem is the explosion of a bomb in the bus station in the town in 1993.[13] I remember the day well as my father was the manager in the branch of the Northern Bank directly adjacent. The bank building was destroyed but thankfully no one was injured in the explosion.

[12] Ibid.
[13] This explosion took place on 23 May 1993. Heaney's connection with the town, from Dr. Kerlin, who had his practice on Broad Street, to his frequent stops there en route to school at St. Columb's, through to 'Two Lorries' is commemorated there today with an installation by the bus station.

GHOSTS 89

I have a photograph of my father standing in the ruins after with a hard hat on and a slight smile on his face, as if none of this was to be taken too seriously, which makes me wonder now if our wry northern humour has its roots in darker places than we like to think. The poem has something of this estranged perspective, beginning as it does with the Belfast coalman flirting with Heaney's mother. Light-heartedly, he asks her would she ever like to go to cinema, which allows Heaney play with the idea of film as a covering and a projection. Both are ghost-like, as is the white ash that is left on the stove and grate. Like many of Heaney's vision poems, 'Two Lorries' begins and ends in rain, the squall of circumstance cleared for a moment for the apparition of some deeper truth. This happens now as the reduction of the bus station to 'dust and ashes' opens the door to

> …a vision of my mother,
> A revenant on the bench where I would meet her
> In that cold-floored waiting-room in Magherafelt,
> Her shopping bags full up with shovelled ashes.[14]

She is mute, but part of a sequence that Heaney thought of as the human chain, the idea for which is there in the image of death as

> …a dust-faced coalman
> Refolding body-bags, plying his load
> Empty upon empty[15]

'Two Lorries' ends with a familiar invocation to instruct the dead to take shape in a certain form, which is the founding principle of Heaney's ghostly poetry. Words are the link between this world and another as words alone survive. In the earlier poems Heaney knew how to raise the dead but was uneasy of their speech. He listened for voices and looked for signs. In the last poems he bids them speak and act directly, a master

---

[14] 'Two Lorries', *SL*.   [15] Ibid.

of his medium, perhaps as he had always been, but less shy now to show it.

> So tally bags and sweet-talk darkness, coalman.
> Listen to the rain spit in new ashes
> As you heft a load of dust that was Magherafelt,
> Then reappear from your lorry as my mother's
> Dreamboat coalman filmed in silk-white ashes.[16]

By this reckoning, Heaney's late poetry is an art of departure, not arrival. The speaker is there with the dead, and near one of them, as the pun on 'filmed' allows. This Heaney is director of a production he knows he will join on stage at the end, the 'dreamboat' a movie star and Charon's packet, the passage of time and the river Styx one and the same. The allusion is there too in 'A Sofa in the Forties', a poem of family gathering that charts the journey of life from memory to poetry. The substance of this work is a portrait of Heaney and his siblings playing on the settee. As the poet remembers lining up on some imaginary journey, the floor begins 'to wave' and he wonders is it a

> Ghost-train? Death-gondola? The carved, curved ends,
> Black leatherette and ornate gauntness of it
> Made it seem the sofa had achieved
> Flotation.[17]

One of the pleasures of reading these poems closely as late works is hearing the echoes of what came before. Heaney was steeped in Dante, whose poetry opened the door from Mossbawn to purgatory. Now there is the ghost of another image in the background, the Venetian gondola another version of the ghost ship that always signals death. That Heaney writes this image into childhood shows how in the later poems all times exist altogether all at once. The poet's vision of the moment is that of a portal, which channels the remembered and the read into a flickering

---

[16] Ibid.   [17] 'A Sofa in the Forties', SL.

form that has the quality of cinema as much as poetry. The children take their seats as if at the picture house, led by one playing the fireman driving his truck:

> ...We were
> The last thing on his mind, it seemed; we sensed
> A tunnel coming up where we'd pour through
> Like unlit carriages through fields at night,
> Our only job to sit, eyes straight ahead,
> And be transported...'[18]

These kaleidoscope lines are a flicker of allusion, to Heaney's own poetry and to others. Philip Larkin's 'Whitsun Weddings' hovers in the background of the train journey, just as the word 'transported' carries the weight of both history and mystery.[19] I have described these late poems as watercolours and as cinema, and both terms suggest the visual apparition of overlaid imagery, all of which gives the reader a sense of uncertain landscape, described in plain language. The propulsion for these poems is part of their construction too, the moving image key to the generation of artistic perception.

Heaney had always been on the move, in his poems and in his life. The poetic journeys were often freighted with death, even going back to his childhood, even if they often found room for pleasure too. The summary of these fatal landscapes is the underground transit of 'District and Circle', which mines into the ground below London in a journey that comes close to Heaney's ghostly core.[20] I write close and not complete as 'District and Circle' is not a final poem, like 'The Riverbank Field'. It is a trial-piece and a timepiece, a clattering, full-speed approach to what Heaney discovered he could only see by reverie and slow walking. 'District and Circle' is a purgatory in which the soul is still embodied

---

[18] Ibid.
[19] Philip Larkin (1922–1985) was an English poet and librarian, who worked for five years from 1950 in Queen's University Belfast.
[20] The District and Circle lines share tracks and stations in the London Underground. The modern day Circle line was originally one of two separate railways in central London, the other being the Metropolitan. Heaney favoured the idea of the underground loop as a metaphor for the transit between life, death, and return.

and the poem is unusual in the attention it gives to touch and sensation. The underground is the perfect stage for this preliminary drama, its circle line a promise of return in keeping with the poem's hesitancy to mistake the rituals of motion with those of departure. The poem is choreographed as a meeting between the speaker and his father, the 'watcher' who follows him down towards the platform, 'our traffic... in recognition'.[21] Of what we are not told, except for the suggestion that a meeting with this dream companion would be final. For the moment, the two shadow each other, the next world guarded behind the 'dreamy ramparts'[22] of the escalators, up and down. The other people in the poem are double too, some quotidian, some suggestions of something else,

> A crowd half straggle-ravelled and half strung
> Like a human chain, the pushy newcomers
> Jostling and purling underneath the vault...[23]

Even underground the images of water retain, that 'purling' coming up much later again in 'The Eelworks' when Heaney remembers his youth by Lough Neagh. Heaney's ghosts are a summons of the elements and the fear of 'District and Circle' is its climate-controlled interior, the platform and the carriage removed from the province of the overground. Still, the poem tries to lift the speaker above the dismal furrow of 'roofwort' and 'planted ball', 'buoyed'[24] by the moment before the train moves, everyone alert to the acceleration.

> So deeper into it, crowd-swept, strap-hanging,
> My lofted arm a-swivel like a flail,
> My father's glazed face in my own waning
> And craning...
>
> And so by night and day to be transported
> Through galleried earth with them, the only relict

---

[21] 'District and Circle', *DC*.   [22] Ibid.   [23] Ibid.   [24] Ibid.

Of all that I belonged to, hurtled forward,
Reflecting in a window mirror-backed
By blasted weeping rock-walls.
Flicker-lit.²⁵

Revelation can be imagined as a judgement day of epic proportion. Here it is a quieter recognition that the generations pass in each other's faces, familiarity an admission of the individual's place in the greater sequence. Heaney sees this in flashes in 'District and Circle', the summoning images rising from the dark, the weeping walls a premonition of loss. There is courage in this writing, and a willingness to see oneself as already a shade while still alive. The late poetry is so unusual in its moving beyond the idea of death as an unknown, the late poet constructing landscapes in which he is his own ghost, his words, ideas, and feelings watermarked with a mortal register.

The poem that captures this transition best is the one that recounts Heaney's most traumatic experience of all, his stroke, which he suffered in 2006.²⁶ In Donegal with Marie, Heaney later remembered the event as frightening and affirming, his helplessness in the ambulance as he was taken to Letterkenny hospital a reminder of the love that he and Marie had for each other. She sat with him on the bumpy journey in the back of the ambulance, and her near distance, each strapped into seat and stretcher, made an impression on him that never left the poetry after. 'Chanson d'Aventure' is a love song and a death song, a poem that takes its place in an artistic sequence that extends from classical Greece to contemporary Donegal. The poem's form too is expansive. Its title refers to a medieval mode in which the poet has an unexpected adventure in a rural place, which is sometimes erotic. That stretches it a bit in this case, but the bridge between the old style and the old poet is John Donne's meditation on love and spirit, 'The Ecstasy', two lines of which preface Heaney's poem.

---

²⁵ Ibid.
²⁶ Heaney recalled the events around his illness with wry humour, writing 'I must be the only man who got his first tracksuit thanks to a stroke'. To Denis O'Driscoll, 31 August 2006, *LSH*.

Love's mysteries in souls do grow,
But yet the body is his book.[27]

The correspondence between soul and body is so much the subject of Heaney's later poems that the people and places he describes radiate with it. Donne's poem is an exploration of the possibility of unity between two souls in physical love. It is a seduction and a philosophy, all built on conditions of culture and environment. In Donne, the riverbank is 'like a pillow on a bed',[28] the movement of soul a 'flow',[29] as it is so often in Heaney. There is a similar lightness too, which suggests Donne as one of the voices in Heaney's ear as Heaney wrote his poems of lift and flight,

> On man heaven's influence works not so,
>   But that it first imprints the air;
> So soul into the soul may flow,
>   Though it to body first repair.[30]

Yeats heard this soul music too, the rhythms of 'Sailing to Byzantium' faintly there in a line from Donne to Heaney, all sharing the idea of art as a transaction between consciousness and form. Donne, like Yeats and Heaney, realized that the apparition of soul was a matter for the air, and as transitory. All three had a different attitude to what this meant at different times in their poetry. In Donne it is seductive; in Yeats it is confirmation of his superiority to see it; in Heaney it is secular revelation, wry and poignant. Heaney dressed his art in motley, building to allusion by the general assembly of the everyday moment; however, the circumstances were extraordinary. This, perhaps, was a skill learned in the extremities of the north, and a kind of keeping going that had different outcomes for the poetry as age and overwork took their toll. There are other layers to the poem too, as with Heaney's allusion to the painter

---

[27] 'Chanson d'Aventure', *HC*.   [28] John Donne, 'The Ecstasy'.
[29] Ibid.   [30] Ibid.

Barrie Cooke's 'god beams',[31] the intensity of which is there in the look he and Marie share as they race along.

> Strapped on, wheeled out, forklifted, locked
> In position for the drive,
> Bone-shaken, bumped at speed...
>
> Everything and nothing spoken,
> Our eyebeams threaded laser-fast, no transport
> Ever like it until then, in the sunlit cold
>
> Of a Sunday morning ambulance...[32]

'Chanson d'Aventure' is a poem of incapacity obsessed with motion, images of which move through the poem in wheels and bumps. The preparation is conscious for its later lines, which describe the experience of rehabilitation after the stroke. This is a poem of aftermath, the poet the watchman of his own disorder. Where Yeats forestalled this decline by sealing the present in a golden statue, Heaney looks to the broken outlines of Greece for solidarity.

> The charioteer at Delphi holds his own,
> His six horses and chariot gone,
> His left hand lopped
>
> From a wrist protruding like an open spout,
> Bronze reins astream in his right, his gaze ahead
> Empty as the space where the team should be,
>
> His eyes-front, straight-backed posture like my own
> Doing physio in the corridor, holding up
> As if once more I'd found myself in step
>
> Between two shafts, another's hand on mine,
> Each slither of the share, each stone it hit
> Registered like a pulse in the timbered grips.[33]

---

[31] 'Chanson d'Aventure', *HC*.   [32] Ibid.   [33] Ibid.

The forms of stone and water shape so much of Heaney's poetry it should not be surprising they finally shape his sense of himself. Reduced by time and circumstance, the charioteer has become his bare self, his connection to the outside world expressed in imaginative gesture, the 'open spout' and 'reins astream'[34] like the fountains of an earlier Yeats, the symbols of life. Meaning is in the looking, and what Heaney sees is a physical stance that suggests spiritual presence. This is as much as the late poetry hopes for. There are no monuments but moments, the poem brought back to focus by the bumping hand on memory's plough, his senior's touch guiding him through the stony field. 'Chanson d'Aventure' is the poetic equivalent of Heaney's life flashing before him, and it comes to rest in a premonition of the final journey, when what is past becomes present, the forward motion of life bent into a circle. Previously, Heaney had used a word like pulse for the description of light from a comet. The augur suggested some great change had arrived, and even here, down to earth, the poet flat on his back and then arisen, the word catches a specific point of transition, a late phase before death.

Many of the late poems take this moment as their subject. Its coordinates are the meeting between body and soul that allows the brief visualization of both, in concert but not the same. Heaney looked for these episodes throughout his writing. 'Station Island' is the classic example, William Carleton, James Joyce, and the rest appearing in shimmering sequence. There are many more, the elegies for his family another rich resource of present memory. As much as anything the tone changes in the later poems, which have a calmness about them in keeping with Heaney's commitment to hold steady, whatever comes. Grace is another word that fits, complimentary to the openness Heaney maintained to the shades he summoned. 'Bodies and Souls' is one example, wondering if the afterlife will be like following Jim Logue, his old school caretaker, as he makes his night rounds, Logue the

> Glimmerman of dorms and silent landings,
> Of the refectory with its solid, crest-marked delph,
> The ground-floor corridor, the laundry pile

[34] Ibid.

And boots tagged for the cobbler. Was that your name
On a label? Were you a body or a soul?³⁵

The question implies the disorientation that attends life's changing states. There are many similar moments in poems about Heaney's father, especially as his father shrunk into himself, as one poem has it. There are other times too when these scenes of the ordered past become chaotic, and dangerous. 'Bodies and Souls' is the past as a list, the caretaker like the poet in that he finds a place for everything when no one else is there. This is an operation of the dark, after hours and unseen. If it is not done, then the relationship with the dead, and with the past more generally, becomes problematic. 'Bodies and Souls' closes with an image of a piano played badly by a schoolboy, the 'savagery' of the 'music going wrong' a suggestion that the teacher gives the boy's hands a rap. What begins as an account ends in disquiet, death too quick and close. This is a common transition in the later poems, which combine the old fascination with the handmade and close-to-hand with a deepening anxiety over death. This panorama of memory and experience is the preparatory ground for a further change, which is the acceptance of death, and the dead. Less now are poems haunted by the unsettled past, the Troubles a more distant source of the mutilated forms that emerged in his imagination.

Even so, there is a book to be written in Heaney's use of the word 'wound', which was at once a physical and a psychic mark, deep and raw. It is the summary of Heaney's understanding of history as it is experienced in the contemporary, and the preliminary to poetry, which is its balm. Earlier it was painful and forbidding. Later it was capable of ministry and cure, a process that was one with Heaney's increasing sense of his own mortality. To go further, Heaney's imagination of the reconciled closed a social wound that changed fundamentally his description of the Derry landscape he came from. This remained a process until the end, and one of the reasons to read the late poems is to observe a new world of language, place, and memory come into being, such as it does in 'Damson', which is a panorama and a prologue for that great late

---

³⁵ 'Bodies and Souls', *EL*.

work, 'The Riverbank Field'. 'Damson' is the kind of poem whose first assembly seems all too familiar. It refers to a type of plum that is grown in the garden and made into jam. Heaney's poetry is replete with these domestic images, and sometimes to surfeit. His estrangement from his previous practice begins with the first word, which hails three lines of bloody action,

> Gules and cement dust. A matte tacky blood
> On the bricklayer's knuckles, like the damson stain
> That seeped through his packed lunch.[36]

'Gules' derives from an Old French word, which described a shade of heraldic red. It can also mean a throat, or a fur for the neck, the three combining in the poem's thick air, an atmosphere that clots the language into sticky groups of association. This is the poem as an act of reduction, images boiled down to their essence, from which new matter is made. In this case the bricklayer's raw knuckles open a portal to the underworld of matter-made memory:

> Wound that I saw
> In glutinous colour fifty years ago—
> Damson as omen, weird, a dream to read—
> Is weeping with the held-at-arm's-length dead
> From everywhere and nowhere, here and now.[37]

Heaney's summons of time and place marks a major departure in the later poems. Earlier the dead came in vision, erupting quickly and gone just as soon, the poem left in stunned reflection. Here and now the dead are everywhere among the living. The lesson learned is to live with them, poetry the equivalent of the builder's trowel,

> Its edge and apex always coming clean
> And brightening itself by mucking in.[38]

---

[36] 'Damson', *SL*.   [37] Ibid.   [38] Ibid.

The roadside dirt that fouled the dead of the Troubles poems is ditched for the collective work of communal labour, such as happens in 'Human Chain'. Heaney had always an eye for the cooperative work of turf cutting and cattle dealing. It turns now to the translation of these intimacies into a social ethic of witness and inclusion, which is the practice of transcendence. The first step is to see the dead as they are, unsettled.

> Ghosts with their tongues out for a lick of blood
> Are crowding up the ladder, all unhealed,
> And some of them still rigged in bloody gear.[39]

The next is to consider how to respond, like 'Odysseus in Hades lashing out', or

> ...not like him—
> Builder, not sacker, your shield the mortar board—
> Drive them back to the wine-dark taste of home,
> The smell of damsons simmering in a pot,
> Jam ladled thick and steaming down the sunlight.[40]

As with so many of Heaney's late poems, the light of earlier works and words breaks through. 'Damson' ends with an echo of the poem 'Sunlight', Heaney's memorial for his aunt Mary. That poem was published in *North*, the mid-seventies collection that faced the upsurge of violence with measured severity. Its panorama was the Atlantic archipelago of early-modern raiders whose Viking attacks had shaped Ireland a millennium before. It was the predicate too of Heaney's interest in the cultures of human sacrifice that preceded Christianity in that northern arc from Ireland to Denmark. 'Sunlight' couldn't be farther from these buried atrocities, the tortured bog bodies given way to love,

> like a tinsmith's scoop
> sunk past its gleam
> in the meal-bin.[41]

[39] Ibid. [40] Ibid. [41] 'Mossbawn 1: Sunlight', *N*.

'Damson' merges the two worlds as if in a lesson learned. The cycle of active violence was coming to an end with the publication of *The Spirit Level*, and with it a change from understanding the past as a warning towards thinking of the future as a possibility. That dream of freedom had always been there, if foreclosed by loss and melancholy. Later it is dreamlike, ghostly, and less burdened by its violent archaeology. Heaney's slow movement towards peace was a self-realization that freedom required a letting go not far from death. That ghostliness grows in the later collections, Heaney working with the shades until they are all made of light. He began in typical steadfast fashion with a return to Tollund, that site of familiar barbarity. Earlier Heaney had looked for some deeper human meaning in the killing of a man for the security of society. Now, he wanders further, 'Outside all contention'.[42]

> That Sunday morning we had travelled far.
> We stood a long time out in Tollund Moss:
> The low ground, the swart water, the thick grass
> Hallucinatory and familiar.[43]

That last line captures so much of Heaney's Troubles era poetry. The marking of the local territory with dialect forms carried from home is familiar too, Tollund a place that 'could have been Mulhollandstown or Scribe'.[44] Whereas before that recognition tattooed fatality into the landscape, now it makes for a softer bog-land bed, the comparison opening a horizon of new possibility:

> ...it was user-friendly outback
> Where we stood footloose, at home beyond the tribe,
> More scouts than strangers, ghosts who'd walked abroad
> Unfazed by light, to make a new beginning
> And make a go of it, alive and sinning,
> Ourselves again, free-willed again, not bad.[45]

---

[42] 'Tollund', *SL*.   [43] Ibid.   [44] Ibid.   [45] Ibid.

There is, for all that, a stiltedness in the language that brings the poem to a jarring end. It is as if the conditions for social change are in place without the words catching up. We tend to think of published poems as finished things, dependent as they are on the economy of thought. Here, however, is a work in progress, just like the society it describes. A poem can be of the moment in many ways, and 'Tollund' is as unsure of its new turn as is the poet. Ghostliness is the veil around which to draw this uncertainty, which is void of the gothic that haunted these northern poems previously. The fabric of time is diaphanous, or in Heaney's own luminous term, 'Unfazed by light'.

The question of how to rethread it into some new arrangement of experience remained, and Heaney returned to it in the title poem of *Electric Light*. The suggestion of mechanical illumination hints at his awareness of the staleness of repeating the old poetic tricks. Indeed, the poem begins with a requiem to an old way of writing, a candle lighting the room of a Derry farmhouse like 'a littered Cumae'.[46] The allusion is to one of the earliest and most enduring Greek colonies on the Italian peninsula, which later gifted the Sibylline books to the city of Rome. These words of the female oracles are translated into the childhood memory of his grandmother, who spoke

> In a voice that at its loudest did nothing else
> But whisper.[47]

Left there by his parents for a night, he cries, to her disquiet.

> 'What ails you, child,
> What ails you, for God's sake?' Urgent, sibilant
> *Ails*, far off and old. Scaresome cavern waters
> Lapping a boatslip.[48]

The work in progress is also an approach to an established question from a different angle. If Heaney wondered how to write the future of a world of light, he had first to draw the darkness. Where before he found

---

[46] 'Electric Light', *EL*.   [47] Ibid.   [48] Ibid.

it in the layers down, in bog and marshy field, now he takes to the water, thinking of the association between Sybil and sea, whisper and wave,

> Lisp and relapse. Eddy of sybilline English.
> Splashes between a ship and dock, to which,
> *Animula*, I would come alive in time
> As ferries churned and turned down Belfast Lough[49]

The odyssey takes Heaney across the Irish Sea to London, Larkin, Spenser, and Shakespeare in train as the poet emerges

> From tube-mouth into sunlight,
> Moyola-breath by Thames's 'straunge stronde'.[50]

This is the core of the poem, and a point of departure for the poetry to come. Heaney's shorthand summary of English literary influence on his mental journey from Derry to London is a gathering and a reformation, an awareness that poetry lives in a constellation of connections, none of which are absolute. The awareness of these earlier writers is of a different kind than his relationship with his home place. The line between home, memory, experience, and elsewhere is as rickety and submerged as an underground line, and as circular in exchange (as 'District and Circle' so lightly suggests). It is prone to interruption too, and a change in tack, as Heaney looks for now. Returning to Derry, he remembers himself as if a character from Dickens, his ability to enlighten the source of great expectation.

> If I stood on the bow-backed chair, I could reach
> The light switch. They let me and they watched me.
> A touch of the little pip would work the magic.[51]

---

[49] Ibid.
[50] Ibid. Edmund Spenser (1552/53–1599) was an English poet and colonist of the Munster plantation. Heaney was aware of Spenser's poetry and of his legacy, as he was of other Elizabethan writers: 'I read them first as textbook poetry; they were part of my learning process: finding where I was in the world of culture...You can take pleasure in their verse yet understand that they were racist theorists, contributors to a nascent English imperialism. Edmund Spenser writes a treatise for the elimination of the native Irish: either they can be made English or they can be done away with.' *SS*, 455.
[51] Ibid.

Still, the equation is not quite right. Illumination seems a sleight of hand in face of the physical reality of the remembered past, in this case his grandmother, who kept knitting in the dark, her remains

> The dirt-tracked flint and fissure of her nail,
> So plectrum-hard, glit-glittery, it must still keep
> Among beads and vertebrae in the Derry ground.[52]

Seeing the inner light of things is the practice of poetry itself, an art that Heaney's grandmother showed him as she worked by hand in the dark, as he later set himself to do. The poet never grew out of self-admonishment, and the nail rests as another layer in the local ground of his memory. There is however a distance here, in time and affection. It is often the way in his poetry that the objects that hold their form after use are most often the things that his art cannot transform. They represent alien or immutable fact, and suggest disquiet, the beads and vertebrae a scattered sentence, buried in the ground's continual present. Illumination is a work of the air, and of poetry, and perhaps the last major transition in the work is Heaney's raising of memory and mortality into an atmosphere bound by lesser gravity. His subjects are still serious, but the understanding of their relative place and meaning has shifted drastically. So has their form in words, which explains some of the late books' addiction to the double compound, a construction that can become tiresome from overuse.

The effect has its roots in two traditions, in the Anglo-Saxon and the pastoral, which Heaney cites in one of the poems he wrote about his father's last days, 'Seeing the Sick'. The title has a dual meaning of observation and visitation, both of which shape the poem, which is written in conversation with Gerard Manley Hopkins's 'Felix Randal'.[53] Heaney lifts some of Hopkins's words into his own poem, with common reference to sandals and anointment, and both share an ear for similar phrase, Felix Randal 'big-boned and hardy-handsome'.[54] In Hopkins,

---

[52] Ibid.
[53] Gerard Manley Hopkins (1884–1889) was an English poet and Jesuit priest, who was appointed Professor of Classics at University College Dublin in 1885. He was miserable there and died of typhoid. He is buried in Dublin's Glasnevin Cemetery.
[54] Gerard Manley Hopkins, 'Felix Randal'.

witness and company is a benefit to both parties: 'This seeing the sick endears them to us, us too it endears.'⁵⁵ In Heaney it is too, except that he follows his father as they pass this joint equation, his father become 'Spectral' and a 'Ghost-drover.'⁵⁶ Ghostliness is Heaney's gift in the late poems, the making of a shade the sign of love, except that shade hardly does it as the outline is all bright. In the end he draws his father in sunny aspect,

> His smile a summer half-door opening out
> And opening in. A reprieving light.⁵⁷

The correspondence between light, death, and love represents the most substantial equation that Heaney set himself to address in the late poetry. Its operations change entirely the context and panorama of his writing, and the extension of that writing beyond the moment of its making. Heaney's ghosts are not hauntings but presences, and parts of a landscape that is changed in its dimensions by their apparitions. This was true earlier in Heaney's Troubles poems, especially those in which place names become shorthand for atrocity, Tollund, Grauballe, and Nebelgard. Then Heaney tried to make the disfigured dead whole again in body. The later dead are different, their presence heard in the light music of their place and time, which are changed themselves by this addition. Heaney worked at this thought in several poems, considering the weight of a word in place before slowly unrooting it. He does it in 'The Real Names' as a kind of experiment, the lost person Ophelia a literary, rather than a real figure. In doing so he established further that riverbank landscape that became so fundamental to the closing work, the Moyola a Styx without sadness. 'The Real Names' begins with a line from Hamlet, which describes a willow tree bent over the river, from the branches of which Ophelia fell in Shakespeare's work

> from her melodious lay
> To muddy death.⁵⁸

---

⁵⁵ Ibid.   ⁵⁶ 'Seeing the Sick', *EL*.   ⁵⁷ Ibid.
⁵⁸ Shakespeare, *Hamlet*, IV: vii.

Heaney takes the idea and transplants it to the Moyola, except that he changes the tree into a portal of the land and air, not water. The woods around it huddle like passengers waiting for the boatman to the other world,

> Like a line of daunted stragglers bogging down
> In the sedge and glarry wetness of our meadow[59]

This liquid element is framed by a tree with a hollow,

> Two-timing earth and air: corona top
> Of flick-and-shimmer, sprout-and-tremble growth.
> Land and sky assembled themselves round it.[60]

The ghost of Hopkins is there again in the compound descriptions of the land- and skyscape, but the question is less of the presence of other poets than the effect of the change their summons registers in Heaney's own drawing of his Derry mind. He is 'a word away'[61] from a new grammar of place, time, and sensation, the archaeology of which is layered in his reading, his experience, and his memory. In Shakespeare, bad luck is fated, as Queen Gertrude laments:

> One woe doth tread upon another's heel,
> So fast they follow; your sister's drown'd, Laertes.[62]

In Heaney there is no submergence but absorption. If 'The Real Names' is a preparatory sketch for the sensory and environmental dimensions of this landscape of the afterlife, 'St Kevin and the Blackbird' is the portrait of its philosophy and belief. The two poems share an interest in trees and rivers, two common co-ordinates of Heaney's later writings. The subject of 'St Kevin and the Blackbird' is the story of the religious in whose supplicant hands a bird made its nest. Moved to concern, the saint remained in place,

---

[59] 'The Real Names', *EL*.   [60] Ibid.   [61] Ibid.
[62] Shakespeare, *Hamlet*, IV: vii.

> and, finding himself linked
> Into the network of eternal life,
> Is moved to pity: now he must hold his hand
> Like a branch out in the sun and rain for weeks
> Until the young are hatched and fledged and flown.[63]

The blackbird is transport to another form beyond human experience, a distribution that Heaney had experimented with before in more tortured form in *Sweeney Astray*. 'St Kevin and the Blackbird' maps carefully the pains of the body on earth, the saint's suffering a submission to gravity. The consequence of his act of radical empathy is his translation of self to some other zone beyond the individual:

> Alone and mirrored clear in love's deep river,
> 'To labour and not to seek reward,' he prays,
> A prayer his body makes entirely
> For he has forgotten self, forgotten bird
> And on the riverbank forgotten the river's name.[64]

Together these late poems draw a panorama of sight and soul that lifts the work up and away from the rootedness of the earlier collections. It is true that Heaney was alert in his poetry to the inner light of what was around him. Even the darkest moments had their hints of illumination, and a hope for more. Nearer the end, as he was aware, Heaney remade his Derry hinterland as a site of the unknown future. This is no small gesture for a land and water so deeply inscribed by the sharp force of violent history. Holding that in mind while seeing something through and beyond it was a question of perspective, which Heaney achieved by shifting himself into the world of ghosts.

We have arrived now at the end of things, the ground drawn, the river in sight, and the sky open overhead, as it often is on a summer's day on the Lough near Bellaghy, high cloud scudding off towards the Irish Sea. Remarkable among it all is the absence of fear or sadness in the art.

---

[63] 'St. Kevin and the Blackbird', *SL*.   [64] Ibid.

There is determination, certainly, and at times a dogged perseverance, but no doubt or questions as to what comes next, even if it is nothing. In 'The Poet's Chair', Heaney had addressed Leonardo Da Vinci's idea that the sun had never seen a shadow. He took the implications of this observation into his poetry further than Da Vinci might have imagined, creating a ghost world that had the bright aspect of a Derry Elysium. The idea was there in his reading of Virgil, in his experience, and in his determination to find a new mode that did not do away with the old, a depth without burden. He made this afterlife a version, as he did of the classical texts, a place made from his constant reworking of word, place, and weather. Heaney's Roman Moyola is a crossing towards a place none of us know, except as the outline of absence. What presence then to fill the dark with light, the river with water, the fields with golden sun, the poet a ghost within, the spirit a tremor in the eternal spring, some day to return.

Late Heaney. Nicholas Allen, Oxford University Press. © Nicholas Allen 2026.
DOI: 10.1093/9780198985419.003.0004

5
The Riverbank Fields

By the late work, the riverbank had become Heaney's sovereign territory. He had long noticed the significance of this marginal terrain between land and water, between the conditions of the here, the now, and the past and future, in other writers. 'The Strand at Lough Beg', which stands as one of his greatest, and saddest, poems begins with an epigraph from Dante's *Purgatory*:

> *All round this little island, on the strand*
> *Far down below there, where the breakers strive*
> *Grow the tall rushes from the oozy sand.*[1]

The scene echoes through Heaney's poetry, from the cold waters of Lough Derg to the softer channels of the Moyola. Constant is the question of where life begins and ends, or better to say of where it continues and in what form after death. Sometimes Heaney looked for this animation in fish and bird and tree. Sometimes he wrote it through the land and waterscape itself, the air a medium to light the whole. In this mode he imagined the river as a portal and less a transit, a depth to be looked into and through rather than a current to carry him elsewhere.

That idea was partly local in orientation. The waterlands that Heaney grew up in are slow-moving places, bound by sedge and bog. The Moyola is the last tributary of a series of streams that merge in the pooling waters before Lough Neagh, that silver inland sea that sits at the heart of the north. Heaney knew the territory in detail and panorama. He walked the evening fields by the Lough with his father as they checked on their cattle. He saw the whole as he looked back from the Glenshane Pass, the road he travelled regularly to and from school in

[1] 'The Strand at Lough Beg', *FW*.

Derry. From the top on a clear day the north is visible from the Sperrins to the Mournes, Lough Neagh a dull glitter to the right, the Antrim Coast a level of cloud by the hump of Slemish, where St Patrick preached. The symbolic dimensions of these territories take a lifetime to accrue, but their outlines are sketched early, in the late day lowing of the cattle, or the airless transport of a regional bus. Finding their corollaries in the literatures of other times and places is a step further into their depths, and Heaney spent a lifetime of reading and writing to find echoes of his remembered places in his imagined. Dante offered one structure, in elegy. Gerald Manley Hopkins offered another, in solitude, longing, and the embodiment of a desire for spiritual renewal in the touch and feel of the given place. Hopkins did more again, supplying a language of combination that Heaney took up and merged with his own interests in translation and adaptation. After all, besides the poems, some of Heaney's most interesting late work is his versions, of the *Aeneid* and of *Beowulf*.

The late work is unified by Heaney's desire to illuminate his art with an imagery as deep and varied as the lives he sensed within it, human, animal, and arboreal. The river too is live, the Moyola a goddess and a familiar, its waters constant. The thought is contrary to the idea of a river in constant motion, from beginning to whatever end it finds in lake or sea or ocean. For Heaney the river was a water world entered from its banks, looked into and crossed over, but rarely, if ever, followed along. It is of the place as much as the field and sky, its difference its transparency, which Heaney read as a capacity to be in two states at once, visible and immersed. It came to represent for him the space of transition between the here and the hereafter, and was there always, from the beginning to whatever imagined end the poet had the powers to make. To Heaney, the riverbank was the place where landscape, memory, and the ghosts of those who had already passed shared imaginative space. In his late work it is the place of summary and conclusion, of vision and preparation, a mental geography that ranged from the classical world to the quiet stretches of rural Derry. By the riverbank Heaney found a place for them all to be, the watch of the earlier poems given way to the wash of water in time. The effect is to create a panorama in which the whole can be held for a moment and found wanting of but one thing, mortality. It was only at the very end that Heaney found a way to approach this last observation without fear or reservation. That he did so at all is remarkable, the path towards this moment written through the late books in asides and adjustments from *The Spirit Level* to the *Human Chain*.

That is, of course, to look back. Death arrives on a date of its own choosing, unbidden unless by tragedy or unwelcome circumstance. It can, however, become a subject of reflection, and where better to see it than by the water. It is remarkable the degree to which Heaney's elegies are dressed in rain and flood, or set by river and sea. The evolution in the late poems was to take these conditions and ground them in a new set of metaphors, Heaney developing a language of premonition by comparison between a revised set of elements in the poetry, and in the world. As with Yeats, stones were in the midst of all, Heaney's attention to grit, gravel, and pebble a measure of the relationship between the worn and the wearing. This is the work of *The Spirit Level*, which patrols the boundaries of the previous work with a new-found, impatient, directness. The question of how to think, and what to say, informs 'The First Words', which has a shortness not often admitted to any of the poems:

> The first words got polluted
> Like river water in the morning
> Flowing with the dirt
> Of blurbs and the front pages.
> My only drink is meaning from the deep brain,
> What the birds and the grass and the stones drink.
> Let everything flow
> Up to the four elements,
> Up to water and earth and fire and air.[2]

Gone here is the sense of origin as a source of clear meaning, as it was, say, with the farmyard pump in Mossbawn. The flow is all wrong, ink running through the water like a stain. There is in this a tiredness and a

---

[2] 'The First Words', *SL*.

self-rebuke, of being drawn into a world of literature that had more to do with its business than its inspiration, a condition that might only have grown worse with the Nobel. Heaney profited from all this too, without doubt, and the poem would stand as a cry of middle-aged crankiness if not for return to the birds, the grass, and stones. Birds sing and grass whispers, but stones are harder to hear, their silences exceeding the span of human life. Derek Mahon had come to this point before in 'The Mayo Tao', a poem about Mahon's self-exile in the west, his company storms and rocks.[3] Heaney's work is less austere, and while similarly self-questioning less cutting in its conclusions. Heaney returns the stones, grass and birds to a condition of flow that is a register of time and experience, memory and feeling.

The key to these transitions is the body, which Heaney draws through the diverse sensations of touch. There is a curious link then between the later elegies and the erotic, which is a connection again to Yeats, if less fervent. In finding new words Heaney found old memories, the effect of which is to populate the later poems with a revised cast of characters acting in a new theatre of place. That place seemed familiar because it had been named so many times before. But read in the shifting light of the late poems, the territory radiating out from rural Derry makes a different impression, like driving beneath the Sperrins in early autumn. Heaney admitted the reader to his process in 'The Gravel Walks', a poem that describes the childhood stretches of the Moyola in a staccato start:

> River gravel. In the beginning, that.
> High summer, and the angler's motorbike
> Deep in roadside flowers...[4]

That first line is a kind of spawning, as if images Heaney had in his deep mind were set to emerge in the poem, the poet waiting by the riverbank, like the angler, to catch the last of what had come before. The sense of lateness is there in the drowsiness of the scene, as it was soon after in

---

[3] 'I have stood for hours / watching a salmon doze in the tea-gold dark, / for months listening to the sob story / of a stone in the road, the best, / most monotonous sob story I have ever heard'. Derek Mahon, 'The Mayo Tao'.
[4] 'The Gravel Walks', *SL*.

Heaney's Nobel speech, Mossbawn a community not fully integrated yet in the modern contrivances of world war, such as 'the engines of the world prepared'.[5] Instead there is a turning and a cycle, a 'whirlpool', over which the 'trees dipped down' and

> The flints and sandstone-bits
> Worked themselves smooth and smaller in a sparkle
> Of shallow, hurrying barley-sugar water
> Where minnows schooled that we scared when we played[6]

The sweetness of this description is all the more for its turn away from the hard shards that littered the riverbeds of the earlier poems, of 'North' and the violent equations between Viking raids and the Troubles, the past a constant din of turbulent waters. Sunlight is often a balm in Heaney's poetry, and its sparkle reflects the gentle scene, the broken stone rubbed smooth in time's current. The gathering fish are premonition too of that later, post-Nobel reflection on Greece, the mullet gathered by Pylos pier. The whole is transformed by the working of men gathering gravel from the riverbank for use in construction, a scene that could have played out for its environmental disturbance but which is instead ghostly, if not foreboding. In its sketch of the landsmen in water it has something of the quality of the later poem, 'The Eelworks', memory not quite in synchronicity with the elements,

> An eternity that ended once a tractor
> Dropped its link-box in the gravel bed
> And cement mixers began to come to life
> And men in dungarees, like captive shades,
> Mixed concrete, loaded, wheeled, turned, wheeled...[7]

There is a sense in these transitional poems of two times at play, one the flat continuance of childhood, a condition Heaney associates with the essential rhythms of Mossbawn and country life, and the other the turn

---

[5] Ibid.   [6] Ibid.   [7] Ibid.

of modernity, in machines and wheels and mixers. There is not necessarily a clash between the two, and one is not the metaphor for the other's deficits as is so often the case in nature poems. Instead they sit beside each other, not antagonistic, but unreconciled, a condition that points to one of Heaney's influences in these observational memories, which is Philip Larkin. The echo of the English poet, who had spent his own time in Belfast, is audible in the second section of 'The Gravel Walks', which sings

> the verity of gravel.
> Gems for the undeluded.[8]

Less deceived are those who can hold what is to hand in a vocabulary shaped for the moment, the shovel digging in its 'plain, champing song'.[9] In this poetry the elements are in sympathy with tools that are a medium to connect to them. Dug up from the riverbed are symbols of this synchronicity, water-smooth stones that represent the currents of deep time the poet thinks of as an extension beyond the bodily present, true gifts of the imagination the return of years of work:

> Beautiful in or out of the river,
> The kingdom of gravel was inside you too—
> Deep down, far back, clear water running over
> Pebbles of caramel, hailstone, mackerel-blue.
>
> But the actual washed stuff kept you slow and steady
> As you went stooping with your barrow full
> Into an absolution of the body,
> The shriven life tired bones and marrow feel.
>
> So walk on air against your better judgement
> Establishing yourself somewhere in between
> Those solid batches mixed with grey cement
> And a tune called 'The Gravel Walks' that conjures green.[10]

---

[8] Ibid.   [9] Ibid.   [10] Ibid.

The three verses are worth quoting in full together for that hesitation in the middle. The first rhymes with lyrical ease, lush with colours drawn from the sky, the evening sun in caramel, the grey in hail, the bright blue of a summer morning in the fish scales. The stones are symbols beyond known time and place, unchanged now by the course of surface water, their experience their form. The second stanza's wavering in the half-rhymes of 'steady' and 'body', 'full' and 'feel' suggests the difficulty of integrating this awareness into bodily form (and it is resonant writing these lines of the similar difficulty Yeats faced in 'Sailing to Byzantium', making the mechanical sing). The words register the weight of moving the wheelbarrow, the motif of carrying common through the later poems, if only as a prelude to lightening the load. To admit the residual hesitation is to be 'shriven' for it, to confess and be absolved, a preparation, as so many times in Heaney's poems, for a further journey to that place between sound and form, once a purgatory and now a resource, a rhythm and a tradition, a quickening like the tune that gives the poem its name.

'The Gravel Walks' does not have the outer confidence of Heaney's Nobel Speech, but is its analogue and preparation, the poet in practice before the revelation of public prose. It is suggestive to think of the two works together and to recognize in their differences Heaney's understanding of their diverse frequencies. It is suggestive too to think how elsewhere in *The Spirit Level* the space-walk could crash to ground, as it does in the elegy for Donatus Nwoga, a Nigerian poet and critic whom Heaney had met as a fellow student in Queen's. 'A Dog was Crying Tonight in Wicklow Also' is based on an Igbo story, which tells of how humans asked the god Chukwu to relieve them of death as a final state, allowing them instead to migrate into other forms and bodies. Their messenger was a dog, who, distracted, allowed the toad to intervene and tell Chukwu that humans wanted the opposite, for death to be final. This is what happened, the poem a lament for the separation of the living from the dead, and Heaney from his friend. Even in these further circumstances, Heaney wrote his elegy with familiar sites in mind, the dog delayed by barking 'from the far bank of a river'.[11] The fatality of the

---

[11] 'A Dog was Crying Tonight in Wicklow Also', *SL*.

poem is the separation of 'great loves',[12] a theme that gives these poems of leaving and loss emotional and personal depth. This is in keeping with Heaney's summons of himself as a ghost, a walking elegy for the people he left behind. These other presences, as he will later call them, people 'The Walk' and 'The Sharping Stone', the two poems in *The Spirit Level* that bring all the elements together, Marie Heaney and her father on both sides of the river, Heaney somewhere between.

Love, then, is the binding element of these riverbank poems, without which the poems would be studies in the unknowable. By this point Heaney had established his intimacy with place, the townlands around Mossbawn a landscape flinted with experiences of Belfast, Dublin, Wicklow, America, Greece, and the many other places he travelled. He had also written beautifully of his mother and father, as he would do later of his brother, his wife, his children and his grandchildren. 'The Walk' and 'The Sharping Stone' are steps across this river of time, moving as they do to a new and airy freedom. 'The Walk' is a sonnet-pair and a reflection, the first set in childhood, the second as an adult, two songs of innocence and experience, but not quite, the language of the elements sown through both, the joint approach to the present subtly rewritten. 'The Walk' is in this sense that curious late Heaney poem, a premonition dressed as a memory and given shape by a changing language that fits time's new folds. This is an art of accumulated experience, which is a mark of Heaney's intention to gather himself and go again throughout his late career, a resolution possible to overlook in repetitive word play, or the too obvious attachment to Hopkins and Old English. Hopkins is there in the unexpected form of the first word of 'The Walk', after which the poem opens out into a portrait of the past that is also the priming of a new canvas. The words are, as always, beautiful, Heaney's attention to the hedgerows a delight, and a distraction from the new way in which he was beginning to build the mental frame of reference around them.

> ...When we stepped out
> Cobbles were riverbed, the Sunday air

[12] Ibid.

> A high stream-roof that moved in silence over
> Rhododendrons in full bloom, foxgloves
> And hemlock, robin-run-the-hedge, the hedge
> With its deckled ivy and thick shadows—
> Until the riverbed itself appeared,
> Gravelly, shallowy, summery with pools,
> And made a world rim that was not for crossing.[13]

What appears at first to be a certain place is subtly anything but. The path from the farmyard out is a subterranean river of stones, an underworld some of whose flowers, like foxglove and hemlock, are deathly. It appears that Heaney has crossed into the land of the dead, across the sunlit river the other side of which is present life. The 'world rim' reminds of the 'hammered curve'[14] in 'North', Heaney's eye on the far perspective, where the shape of the world in space is visible. That darkness beyond is where Heaney sets himself to walk in his Nobel address and looks different detached from the late-twentieth-century fascination with the space race. It bears another, older imprint too, which was Heaney's reading of the *Aeneid*. That interest resulted in the subsequent publication of Heaney's version of Virgil's founding myth, one sequence of which connects to 'The Walk'. In 'The Fields of Light', the sybil asks the celebrated dead of Elysium to direct Aeneas to his departed father, Anchises. To get there Aeneas has crossed 'the mighty waterways', the shades

> singing songs together to Apollo
> Deep in a laurel grove, where the Eridanus
> Courses through on its way to the earth above.[15]

The Greek underworld was a watery place, possessed of rivers and streams, some portals, all boundaries. The equation of water with tears and grief is easily imaginable; the association of death with light is less so, and for a moment 'The Walk' dries up, unable to go further:

---

[13] 'The Walk', *SL*.   [14] 'North', *N*.   [15] *AVI*.

> Love brought me that far by the hand, without
> The slightest doubt or irony, dry-eyed
> And knowledgeable, contrary as be damned;
> Then just kept standing there, not letting go.[16]

The hellish overtone of the damned, dry scene is the berm over which the reader crosses to the poem's second sonnet, which burns everything before it. Where Aeneas risked everything to enter the underworld, much less to return, Heaney risks 'another longshot',[17] which is to imagine his relationship with Marie as fire, not water,

> Two flames in sunlight that can sear and singe,
> But seem like wisps of enervated air,
> After-wavers, feathery ether-shifts[18]

The parched transparency of this imagery leaves the poem in a puzzle, 'apt still to rekindle', but 'none the wiser'.[19] There is pain there too, and a sense of a lingering change in the shared frequency, both of which leave 'The Walk' in a continuing limbo. Resolution requires a different configuration of the senses, poetry an art somewhere between the acts of observation, record, and transfiguration. A version of this surfaces in 'The Sharping Stone', Heaney's poem for his father-in-law, which ferries again between land and water, the riverbank motif this time of a setting off. Not that water comes into the poem immediately. Even by this earlier phase of his later books, Heaney had written so many elegies that the form had become a kind of second nature. His descriptions of the environment around the subject are often so compelling in themselves that they obscure slightly the subject. 'The Sharping Stone' begins self-aware of this accidental transformation, Heaney remembering a gift for his father-in-law that he had forgotten to give, a stone for sharpening knives left in the cedar-wood drawer of an antique chest. The Mediterranean lumber is hint of the poem's Biblical substrate, while the word 'apothecary'[20] hints at a mystery Heaney has failed to fulfil, the stone

---

[16] 'The Walk', *SL*.   [17] Ibid.   [18] Ibid.   [19] Ibid.
[20] 'The Sharping Stone', *SL*.

> Still in its wrapping paper.
> Like a baton of black light I'd failed to pass.[21]

Earlier Heaney would have carried that weight on both shoulders. Later, that 'like' is a slight shrug of the shoulders, an aside worth noting but not fundamental and with something of a rebuke to the habit he was supposed to inherit. The asphyxia of an unchosen inheritance is a challenge to due memorial, which requires another entry. Like Yeats before him, Heaney associated dryness with an aridity of spirit. The stone sits in the 'Airless cinder-depths'[22] of the chest of drawers (and how differently Heaney draws the air here than he does in the first of the two 'Mossbawn' poems), the only way to use it as a summons by its transport into another setting. Turning to memory, Heaney remembers the evening he and Marie lay on their backs in the wet forest, the scene mindful of the soaked woods of Wicklow that are background to 'Exposure'.

> Listening to the rain drip off the trees
> And saying nothing, braced to the damp bark.[23]

Brace is a word for ships and fighting, both of which work their way into the poem through this porous moment. This is a poem for Marie's father, but Heaney can only get to it through images of his own past, which is suggestive of his eddying late style, the words coming to make the work, the process meditative and hypnotic. So the poem approaches its pivot:

> Neither of us spoke. The puddles waited…
> And next thing down we lay, babes in the wood,
> Gazing up at the flood-face of the sky
> Until it seemed a flood was carrying us
> Out of the forest park, feet first, eyes front,
> Out of November, out of middle age,
> Together, out, across the Sea of Moyle.[24]

---

[21] Ibid.   [22] Ibid.   [23] Ibid.   [24] Ibid.

In a poetry of patterned repetition, Heaney makes flight from the myths of the past, gathered in visionary dream. There are echoes in these lines of Moses set adrift in his bed of rushes, of the swans of Lir, and of Sweeney astray in his madness. They combine like propellant, the slow start of the poem giving way to the rush of life, which poetry so often wishes to still. Moderation, it turns out, is no memorial for Marie's father, who found his own second life in older age. To find this medium the poem had to undo its first self of uncertainty. In full spate, Heaney is no longer worried that the vision will overwhelm him, as he used to. Now it is a medium to somewhere else, a far country thought lost but not irretrievable, as the late poetry so often shows. Suitably, 'The Sharping Stone' takes a southern turn in its flight from Ireland, Heaney joining the found and the remembered in his description of a postcard he and Marie had sent her father of an Etruscan couple, modelled in terra cotta. This is a particular medium to meet in, settled clay a more brittle element than the sharping stone. So Heaney can meet his father-in-law in definite form, but on his own terms. Similarly, the Etruscan image suggests a surviving mystery, which drifts off in the poem into other people's language. The idea seems to be that there are, in fact, no settled monuments but symbols and sequences rather, joined in images of flow. So in the picture of the Etruscans Heaney has a premonition of St Kevin, whose protection of the nesting blackbird did not enter Heaney's poetry until years later. The Etruscans are at ease:

> He is all eyes, she is all brow and dream,
> Her right forearm and hand held out as if
> Some bird she sees in her deep inward gaze
> Might be about to roost there. Domestic
> Love, the artist thought, warm tones and property,
> The frangibility of terra cotta...
> Which is how they figured on the colour postcard
> *(Louvre, Département des Antiquités)*[25]

---

[25] Ibid.

For a poetry largely written in English, Heaney's work had always been an act of translation, of himself, and of his time and place. He read other writers to discover variations on this register, each example an attempt to see the self in dimensions that brought millennia together. The early attempts to do this in context of the Troubles caused him difficulty as poems like 'North' and 'Punishment' were read as examples of equation by analogy. Later Heaney found space in the act of comparison itself, the life of the poem in the form of the comparison, not the objects being compared. In a sense this speaks to the words Heaney found for the titles of his last books, in electrification, the underground, the spirit and, most complex of all, the ties that bind us in the figure of a chain. The late poems can be read as an exploration of these psychological transits, so many of which take shape by rivers and their banks, water Heaney's form and medium. 'The Sharping Stone' is a poem like this. Confronted with the definite figure of his father-in-law the poet finds a way to shape a picture of him through his transfiguration into other forms. Heaney's elemental elegies are concerned as much with the moment of transition between two states as they are to represent the nature of those forms themselves. They have humour too, which gives a lightness to these spiritual leavings. The next sequence of 'The Sharping Stone' brings the question of translation directly to the surface:

> He loved inspired mistakes: his Spanish grandson's
> English transliteration, thanking him
> For a boat trip: 'That was a marvellous
> Walk on the water, granddad.' And indeed
> He walked on air himself, never more so
> Than when he had been widowed and the youth
> In him...
> Grew lightsome once again.[26]

That punning 'lightsome' holds so much meaning in Heaney's late work. It is a quality of the unburdened and of the transitional, a ghostliness of the day time with no haunting quality. It is the final knowable state

[26] Ibid.

before we pass into something else and different, an awareness of mortality as a shifting condition without fear of darkness. The gift of luminosity is Heaney's highest compliment. In these poems of landscape and memory, illumination becomes a formal process in itself, a practice whose many rites stretch from the Etruscan to the Irish, all joined in the common concern to see what is around us as immanent and animated on its own terms.

> So set the drawer on freshets of thaw water
> And place the unused sharping stone inside it:
> To be found next summer on a riverbank
> Where scythes once hung all night in alder trees
> And mowers played dawn scherzos on the blades,
> Their arms like harpists' arms, one drawing towards,
> One sweeping the bright rim of the extreme.[27]

The music of these lines is beyond the memory of the person, extending into the memory of place and experience. That motion is the elegy's engine, its propulsion the rhythm of body in time, the hand, the harp, and the scythe all means to establish a tempo from which the words are drawn, like blades. That word comes up in 'Herbal', another verdant late poem concerned with the reconstitution of a past world from the pastoral. It suggests how images of violence linger even in these poems of leaving, the image defused here by the 'drawing' and 'sweeping', the infections of the world remedied by the social habits of domestic practice, such as make for so many of Heaney's poems of rural life. That last curvature has echoes of other poems too, of 'North' again, and of 'Wordsworth's Skates', the collective works their own symphony, the tone lightening as the end nears. A feeling of lift had entered the poetry and in doing so changed Heaney's understanding of its first principles. His late turn towards the classics, to Horace and Virgil, was an act of innovation, the old become new in Heaney's versions of the classical world. This was a place of possibility, lit by the Mediterranean, Heaney's experiences of Greece, and some thought of his earlier reading as a

[27] Ibid.

schoolboy, the *Odyssey* and the *Aeneid* stories of struggle, but also of sun and sea. These between worlds become a door to the future opened by Heaney's elegies for the past, the poems better built now to shift the weight. 'Anything Can Happen' is in this mode. Based on Horace's *Odes* it is a song and an instruction, an invitation and a statement. It measures in miniature the major forces that shifted in Heaney's poetry since the beginning. 'Anything Can Happen' is a poem with its own weather and myths, Heaney pulling the strings of a Roman god, Jupiter throwing his lightning

> Across a clear blue sky. It shook the earth
> And the clogged underearth, the River Styx,
> The winding streams, the Atlantic shore itself.[28]

The earth is a line drawn between the overworld and the under, the poem a thread like a river that winds between. The impression is of an airy skyscape, of a kind with Heaney's poetry of the west coast of Ireland, the buffets of wind surprising consciousness into a heightened form of awareness. That 'clogged' suggests that many souls, or presences as Heaney has it later, have been waiting for exactly such a clearance. They are the 'overlooked', who Heaney often turned to in his Roman versions. He was aware of the imperial, as the imaginative, aspects of Horace and then of Virgil, and his versions of Latin poetry often carry these asides. The attitude is reminiscent of the earlier Belfast poet Louis MacNeice's 'Autumn Journal', when he imagined the workings of classical Greece:

> And when I think I should remember the paragons of
>   Hellas I think instead
> Of the crooks, the adventurers, the opportunists,
> The careless athletes and the fancy boys,
> The hair-splitters, the pedants, the hard-boiled sceptics…
> and lastly I think of the slaves.

[28] 'Anything Can Happen', *DC*.

> And how anyone can imagine oneself among them I do
> not know;
> It was all so unimaginably different
> And all so long ago.

Heaney read MacNeice closely, and also found resource in ancient texts. Heaney, again, was invested in the act of translation, more than he was in the subject of discussion. He was aware of both, but the attraction to Horace, as to Virgil, was the invitation to draw layers on a canvas the borders of which came closer and closer to the map of his own imagination. Heaney sketched the landscapes and myths of classical literature over the contours of his own imagined place with a view to liberating both from the politics of the moments that made them. Another of his contemporaries had tried this too. The end of Friel's *Translations* ends with a vision of the *Aeneid* in light of the 1798 rebellion that fades into darkness. Heaney worked closely with Friel in the Field Day Theatre Company, where they were joined by Heaney's old school friend, Seamus Deane.[29] Heaney shared his Field Day colleagues' commitment to the unheard and misrepresented. Heaney, however, found a different way to integrate the classical world into the present by giving poetry an agency preserved for the divine, and art a responsibility to see, like MacNeice, the full and often unjust mechanics of the world:

> Ground gives. The heaven's weight
> Lifts up off Atlas like a kettle-lid.
> Capstones shift, nothing resettles right.
> Telluric ash and fire-spores boil away.[30]

As a rallying call for freedom this is complicated. It depends on water for its progress, enlightenment a kind of continuing rumble where things are constantly unsettled. The association of this with a burning away of the earth gives the poem a scorched, uncomfortable ending. It is

---

[29] Seamus Deane (1940–2021) was a friend of Heaney's since St. Columb's days, and Heaney dedicated the poem 'Singing School' to him. He was an academic and a writer, and a great encouragement to me. *Reading in the Dark* is a classic of Irish writing.

[30] 'Anything Can Happen', *DC*.

as if Heaney, in working through the elements from one to the other, was caught midway, not sure how to finish the formula. The poem could see how things might change for the better, but was not ready yet to say what better might be. This was a familiar problem for Heaney, who was not given to advice. Still, the awareness of a need to speak, and the practice of a renewed language capable to accommodate hope and testimony, drove such poems to the surface.

Another way was to translate the home place again, to walk to the riverbank in search of another reflection, this one capable of carrying earth, water, and sky before it. This required new exploration, and a new language that was not always ready to be found. The revised approach can be read in a poem like 'Moyulla', which is a sedimental layering of memories mediated through the flow of the pebbly, shallow River Moyola. Now, near the end, the river emerges as the last tributary of the poet's imagination, a flow as yet unregulated by the sudden rush of interlocking images. At first reading, 'Moyulla' echoes earlier poems like 'Anahorish' and 'Broagh', concerned as they were with the names of places, and the sonic power of local attachment. 'Moyulla' has this aspect too, except that historical time in the poem is foreshortened, the poet's life, and not his community's, the key register of the past. 'In those days',[31] it begins, but deceptively, the rhetorical flourish of the storyteller giving way to a more personal intimacy, an image of the female river sliding into an image of Marie Heaney, in from the garden. There follows a sequence of thoughts that tumble out before the poem gathers itself for the final lines, which invite the reader to walk in the water one day, 'upstream, in the give and take'. The sense of life as struggle is real in the poem, sat uneasily beside its strange and failed eroticism, the milky pollution of the recently built dairy factory a fascination for the young boy and the later man.

Heaney struggled with the balance between these poems, caught as he was between recording life as it was and how it might yet become. As Marie Heaney's apparition suggests, he was aware too that he wrote within a social frame the description of which was complicated for a

---

[31] 'Moyulla', *DC*.

poet whose every expression of intimacy was in the public eye. Metaphorical abstraction was one method, as led to the overflow of 'Moyulla'. A refusal to engage was another, as in a poem like 'The Birch Grove', which is written in 'earshot of river water' but which ends with its male speaker paraphrasing Joseph Brodsky's Nobel speech that 'If art teaches us anything…it's that the human condition is private'.[32] The problem remained then of how to integrate a new and luminous sense of the world as it darkened with a poetic language that did not excavate or expose. Earlier, Heaney paid forensic attention to the bog bodies. Dissatisfied now with the human shape of metaphors trying to catch the shape of a language after life, Heaney turned to the river as a place of other presences. If the ghosts of his memory were not enough, perhaps a premonition of place as time might offer another canvas. It is some magic in a poem like 'At Toomebridge' to illuminate the Bann's departure from Lough Neagh as a transformation. The river there is wide mouthed and slow, channelled in concrete and toothed by the eel fishery's rusting span. It meanders out round a bend by Church Island, marshy and sodden, the province of migratory ducks and swans, before it heads off to the northern sea. Flattening the landscape allowed Heaney to imagine the area again, history a matter of the air now, of spirits and divination; the centuries-long shadows of injustice, insurrection, and retribution fade in the opened air.

Heaney's molecular perspective suggests a breaking down and a reconstitution, which returns him to a different starting point than 'Moyulla'. There he was the young boy wide-eyed on the riverbank. 'At Toomebridge' his fascination is with the eel drawn up from the dark of the water, poetry a net fine enough to catch even the most miniature presence of historical tension in the landscape, however hard it is to land. Considered like this, the riverbank becomes site of a revised form of writing, an elevated perspective on the sky and on the water, a fulcrum around which everything turns. Some of the most playful waterside poems have this aspect, as does 'Perch', which observes the fish

---

[32] 'The Birch Grove', DC.

> Guzzling the current, against it, all muscle and slur
> In the finland of perch, the fenland of alder, on air
> That is water, on carpets of Bann stream, on hold
> In the everything flows and steady go of the world.[33]

The melancholy have it too, as does the elegy for Rory Kavanagh, 'Clonmany to Ahascragh':

> And if ever tears are to be wiped away,
> It will be in river country,
> In that confluence of unmarked bridge-rumped roads
> Beyond the Shannon…[34]

That small lift of the bridge over the country road is an elevation the late poems allow like a step into the sky. There is an energy to these images that comes from a different source than the digging and the farm work that is the earlier base layer. The ground beneath the poet's feet is a line of horizon between water and sky, a flat earth that is border to the infinite above, the moving below. There is an image for this intricacy in Heaney's poem 'A Herbal', which asks

> Where can it be found again,
> An elsewhere world, beyond
>
> Maps and atlases,
> Where all is woven into
>
> And of itself, like a nest
> Of crosshatched grass blades?[35]

That last word suggests the difficulty Heaney had in imagining a pastoral, or a visionary, poetry beyond the conditions of history as he had experienced and understood it. It seems in the end that there was no

---

[33] 'Perch', *EL*.
[34] 'Clonmany to Ahascragh', *EL*. Rory Kavanagh was the son of Heaney's school friend, Des Kavanagh.
[35] 'A Herbal', *HC*.

elsewhere world, but an elsewhere in this world. It too was beyond maps and atlases, being legible in other forms, in the quality of light on a landscape, its weather and, crucially for the poetry, its synchronicity between language and place. The late poetry combines an awareness of the environment as a stage for the passing of all life, regardless. But it is also something more again, an illumination and a radiance that gives the poems new light and setting. Once, Heaney had declared his intent to set the darkness echoing. Having done that, he gathered his soundings and set to illuminate what he had found. He did so in the company of other poets who spoke to him of the under- and the overworlds, the earth a thin line between. After the Nobel he had had little time to absorb all this. Illness changed that, as did a slowing of the body that came with age, and a long overdue effort to curtail his social engagements. This is the late landscape of his versions of Rilke, which were written not long before he suffered his stroke, 'The Apple Orchard' a place such as he might have known in Derry:

> Come just after the sun has gone down, watch
> This deepening of green in the evening sward....[36]

What the reader sees in the fruit trees is the cultivation of 'an inner dark infused' with 'new hope and half-forgotten joys.'[37] The poem pointed Heaney towards a resolve and a recollection that was in search of a new language. He found it in making versions of translations he had collected over the years, from his time as a schoolboy to his semesters in Harvard. Rilke was one resource, his poems a gauze veil between the here, the now and the hereafter, and all at once. Wordsworth was there too, *The Prelude* a manifesto for the writer's lifelong process of self-becoming, while Virgil knit everything together. Heaney had read deeply in David Ferry's translation of the *Eclogues*, which encouraged him to create his own versions in turn. Heaney also embarked on a version of Book VI of the *Aeneid*, which was published after his death. Heaney's familiarity with the songs of farm and field helped him stage the rural as a condition of the underworld that is foundation to human experience at large, in particular

---

[36] 'Rilke: The Apple Orchard', *DC*.   [37] Ibid.

when Aeneas comes upon the subterranean fields by the Eridanus arranged in 'green welcome'.[38] Here are the spirits of dead heroes and poets alike, wanderers and musicians, the fortunate ones gathered in a 'spacious air' that 'sheds brightness'.[39] Here is the seed of Heaney's discovery that the dark has no hold over art's composition of reality, even if the reality of death is unavoidable. Heaney wrote of his later spiritual belief that he believed less in an afterlife than in the after-image of life. These perspectives, from Rilke, Wordsworth, and Virgil, informed a poetry that drew mortality as an alteration of the light. Heaney had a ghost of this idea before, in the Mossbawn elegy for his aunt, perceptive of a 'sunlit absence'.[40] Virgil's underworld is a place where this division between the here and now and the hereafter does not hold. The Eridanus flows upwards to the land of the living, through lush fields attended by spirits. The geography took hold in Heaney's imagination and found expression in 'The Riverbank Field', a poem that brings everything together, late evening by the Moyola an imprint of experience drawn so thin the boundary between this world and another like paper.

The idea brings the reader back to Heaney's beginnings. Once the page was a line like the ground, a skin for the pen to dig through. Later it became a site of reflection, more the surface of a river than the contour of a bog. This brightened the poems, bringing the horizon close and higher, the experience of reading the awareness of an elevation. The mode hardly bears relation to Heaney's previous poems of place and past, which were haunted so often by personal and historical disquiet. To some degree the irony is that Heaney achieved this attitude at exactly a time in which he struggled to find happiness in the wake of his stroke. There is little sense of this in 'The Riverbank Field' unless this last walk by the Moyola is a leave-taking in advance, a final song for a place Heaney carried in his head wherever he went. The poem begins with an invitation to revisit the Loeb edition of the *Aeneid*, by the entrance to the underworld. Heaney is not ready to cede to that place yet. He sets himself instead to 'confound the Lethe in Moyola',[41] walking its banks from Back Park to Upper Broagh. This was long recalcitrant space for

---

[38] *AVI*. [39] Ibid. [40] 'Mossbawn 1: Sunlight', *N*.
[41] 'The Riverbank Field', *HC*.

Heaney, the core of a poetic territory he guarded determinedly for a lifetime, the 'last gh' in Broagh a sound 'strangers found / difficult to manage'.[42] Perhaps intimacy is one of the liberations of late work since death makes friends of us all. The last walk is a rewriting of Heaney's own boundaries, Virgil adapted to the Derry scene,

> Moths then on evening water...
> Midge veils instead of lily beds[43]

The richness of the environment is consummate with its short life, moths and midges on the wing for the shortest of spans. Heaney draws the picture as a portal, the riverbank a place half in and half out of the here and now, the willows by the river 'Elysian-silvered',[44] the grass full grown. Earlier in 'Broagh' he followed a companion whose heel left small puddles in the boggy ground. Now he is alone except for the imagination of fellow spirits, 'To whom second bodies are owned by fate'.[45] The riverbank is leaving and arrival, a motion there like 'District and Circle', the going down a purchase on the rising up. Heaney builds the gesture into the poem, which he orchestrates like a live performance, the version a translation of an ancient rural culture into the present as much as it is a transport of Virgil to the Derry hinterlands.

> And now to continue, as enjoined to often,
> 'In my own words':
> 'All these presences
> Once they have rolled time's wheel a thousand years
> Are summoned here to drink the river water
> So that memories of this underworld are shed
> And soul is longing to dwell in flesh and blood
> Under the dome of the sky.'[46]

A poet's genius, in the end, is not to think thoughts never thought before, or make visible what is less visible to the rest of us. It is in

---

[42] 'Broagh', *WO*. [43] 'The Riverbank Field', *HC*.
[44] Ibid. [45] Ibid. [46] Ibid.

Heaney's case the gift to gather a series of impressions, drawn over time, in a suitable place, a sensation of reading that suggests synchronicity with a reader's own echoing mind. This is perhaps why poets have long been fascinated with images of frequency and impression, as Heaney was with the radio in his childhood. One way to establish this connection is through familiar objects, as Heaney often did. Another, and deeper, is to do it through experiences, many of which are mediated themselves by reading and seeing the work of other poets and artists. Heaney's versions of Virgil are of this order, the coordinates of the Roman world redrawn in the Irish, the one lying over the other like midges on water, briefly. That dome of the sky owes something to Heaney's response to painters too, mindful as he was of Constable's declaration that he learned to see as a painter in the countryside of his childhood. There is no end to these declensions, even as their forms become legible in close, comparative reading. In late Heaney these forms are aesthetic and spiritual, the image an outline for an attitude of light whose shadows suggest depth and context. They are of this world and another, embodied and intimate, desirous of a life the poet knows he too is close to leaving. The riverbank fields are a first place and last to see this, a border and a transit, a look out and a departure, the gathering of decades in one last location.

Late Heaney. Nicholas Allen, Oxford University Press. © Nicholas Allen 2026.
DOI: 10.1093/9780198985419.003.0005

Afterword

Seamus Heaney died in Dublin on 30 August 2013. He had been admitted to hospital the evening previous after a fall. His passing made an immediate impact. Heaney had become a part of the collective imagination in Ireland, his poems long fixtures in schools, his words an arrangement of the national vocabulary, especially when it came to the still recent legacy of peace in the north. His country background too fed into an idea of Ireland as home to a rural and an organic community, his soft voice and his poems for his children and grandchildren security of a certain nostalgia. That underplays the deeply meaningful ways in which Heaney's poems of family, place, and aging resonated with his readers in Ireland and abroad, the poetry a resource in many circumstances, happy or not. Heaney's art had the gift of familiarity, in part because the freight of its complexity was carried by words that slipped solitary from one poem to another, escaping statement. He looked instead for what he called a 'little quickening',[1] that moment when language, memory, and imagination triangulate to gather in an image, a line, and a poem. Heaney felt that his method did not much change across the span of his writing career. I hope I have shown here how it widened and elevated in the last two decades of his life.

For Heaney also thought of endings as beginnings. The companion poem to 'The Riverbank Field' is 'Route 110', which was also published in *Human Chain* and dedicated to the birth of his first granddaughter, Anna Rose. Like 'The Riverbank Field', it proceeds from a reading of Virgil and the underworld to find a path to a future that Heaney knew he would not see, but which he welcomed nonetheless. 'Route 110' is on its surface the bus journey from Belfast to Toome, the young Heaney

---

[1] Interview in the *Toronto Star*, 28 May 2011.

carrying a second-hand copy of *the Aeneid* in his pocket. Along the way, it becomes a meditation on the social nature of the past as a preparation for the future, a panorama of wakes and funerals given way to games and inheritance, the poem set

> Among shades and shadows stirring on the brink
> …waiting, watching,
> Needy…for translation.[2]

For Heaney, in the end, translation is a pattern of time and place lit by lines whose traces are waymarkers for the generations to come. The words of 'Route 110' are dedicated to the future in the figure of his granddaughter

> Like tapers that won't dim
> As her earthlight breaks[3]

Perhaps only late Heaney could risk that last word, with its image of fracture and of arrival. Perhaps only lateness allowed Heaney imagine community as a conversation across time, the presences all here at once, the world restored, as he had imagined of the Greeks in 'Loughanure', by a self-forgetting that was, at last, not a self-denial. In the time since Seamus Heaney's death, his work has remained a familiar presence for many readers. The chorus of *The Cure at Troy* has become a melody of relief for those who think that peace is conflict's inevitable end. Hope and history have their place in Heaney's poetry. The exhaustion that often attended them is less observed in the public construction of Heaney the poet, even as the letters show how worried his family was by his workload and commitments. It is the fate of the poet to be remembered by phrases taken from a life in words, if the poet is lucky enough to be read at all. Heaney had a global audience from near the beginning of his publishing career, an audience that only grew with time. There was no relief and little middle stretch when words, or readers, fell away.

[2] 'Route 110', *HC*.   [3] Ibid.

The years since his death have secured Heaney's immediate reputation. In Bellaghy, Belfast, and Dublin, there are buildings, archives, and exhibitions attached to his name. There are archives of his work in many of the world's leading universities, and in the National Library of Ireland, where his image can be seen beside those of Yeats, Joyce, Beckett and O'Brien.

This is a reflection on Heaney's genius and on the public relationship with art that still marks the island of Ireland as a literate, and literary culture. The historical conditions of language, writing, and the imagination were fraught for centuries in Ireland. The psychological violence of colonization was matched by the depredations of famine, emigration, and language loss. In that vortex literature became an alternative means of representation, each poem, novel, song, and play an act of disunion from systems of domination that extended across the spectrum of religious to political belief. The practice of art is in this context an act of liberation, of the self and of others.

Heaney was concerned with the reflection of words upon each other, in light and shade. Together this might change perspective on the moment to come, as Heaney imagined 'From the Frontier of Writing'.

> as if you'd passed from behind a waterfall
> on the black current of a tarmac road
> past armor-plated vehicles, out between
> the posted soldiers flowing and receding
> like tree shadows into the polished windscreen.[4]

This composite contains many of Heaney's essential qualities, as he came to refine them: flow, reflection, depth, surface, water, and light. In this mid-career poem, the darkness still abides. In the later the light comes to its full. The afterlife of the poems is in this transition, the after words an after world of brightness made from shades. Some others saw this quality in the poet near the end of his life. The painter Colin Davidson prepared for his portrait of Heaney by creating a series of

---

[4] 'From the Frontier of Writing', HL.

sketches that veer between the force of Heaney's forehead, chin, and nose, and the narrowing recess of his eyes, the face like a cross tossed with Heaney's white hair. Davidson's final painting is in oil and magnificent like all his portraits. The sketches, however, catch an image of the poetry as much as the poet, the underlay of light easier to see in the open hand of the conté crayon, guided by the eye of an artist gifted with the attention to see people and things as they are, underneath.

This impulse to discover is what continues to draw such interest in Heaney's letters and his archives, where students and scholars follow the threads of one word or another through manuscripts, pamphlets, essays, and books, the subtle patterns of his work still weaving new bonds between his art and his readers. Certainly, the Heaney of our time already looks different from the Heaney of a decade ago, or before. This is part of a natural process of change in which all works of art engage, and influence. Over time, a literature of statement can diverge from the evolving lexicon of its readers. A literature of suggestion, and even of evasion, can have a different presence, visiting the reader like a shade, a phantom of peripheral vision. I think of several phrases of Heaney's like this, each of which comes to mind in a different place or context. There are words from 'North' and 'The Strand at Lough Beg' that come to mind when I am in the townlands around Magherafelt, or on the beach at Magilligan, the long strand curving right to the narrow mouth of the Foyle and up to the stony pleats of sea cliffs that lead to Inishowen.

There are through ways too, the Moyola a quiet river, unheralded before Heaney found poetry there. It is still a modest landscape, as if the soft refrain of the lyrics has faded into the autumn mists, Lough Neagh a flat mirror that more often reflects the grey light than the bright flash of artistic revelation. This is as it should be. Heaney was a writer of quiet attitude, as were the generations before him and no doubt the generations to follow. It is a quality to consider in a world of climate catastrophe and hyper-violence. Heaney knew alienation and distress. He also knew community and place. It is no coincidence his remedy for these conditions was written in the form of a poem of endurance dedicated to his brother Hugh. 'Keeping Going' is about the necessity of forward motion, even as it admits the journey might return to its beginnings.

The poem is a collage of fragments, some disturbing, some affirming, all wired into Hugh's restless energy, which is his moral gift.

> My dear brother, you have good stamina.
> You stay on where it happens. Your big tractor
> Pulls up at the Diamond, you wave at people,
> You shout and laugh above the revs, you keep
> Old roads open by driving on the new ones.[5]

Hugh is all that his brother is not, loud and gregarious, well known in the town for who he is, not what he does. The two follow parallel lines, Hugh the road, his brother the poem, and both starting in the same place. Where that happens is a shifting site in Heaney's writing. Sometimes it is the farmyard in Mossbawn, sometimes the shallows of the Moyola, sometimes indoors to the crackle of the radio. Later it becomes a condition rather than a place, out west, up north, offshore and, sometimes, in space. The variable gravity of the later poems is a measure of their experiment, the conditions for which Heaney observed in the world around him. That world changed immensely in his lifetime, personally and professionally. The poet changed with it, asking all the while what remained of the old in the new, and what could hope for better. This was a process of endurance and of inspiration, of practice and of enlightenment. It was rooted in the quotidian, durable, worn, and animated by the moment. So many of Heaney's late poems are made of this everyday fabric, which he knit together in a tapestry of time whose material effect was attention to the world as it might yet be, even as it is.

That was difficult work in the north of the Troubles, as it was again for different reasons with sickness and age. Still Heaney invites the reader into intimacy with his poems, even if, as an individual, he remains a strange familiar, known in part by many people but unknown in substance to any but his family and very closest friends. This was how he wanted it, going so far as to pre-empt his biographers with his own account of himself in *Stepping Stones*, the series of interviews he curated

---

[5] 'Keeping Going', *SL*.

with Dennis O'Driscoll. However this attitude will endure into the future, there remains the question of how, and why, we read Heaney today, and tomorrow. Of all the imaginable answers to this question, perhaps the late work provides a key. At its best it finds new life in the familiar, even as life's prospect shortens. Art composed near the end of a life is associated with trial and intensity. Certainly, Heaney had that in his personal life, particularly after his stroke and the occasional depression that followed it. But in the work, there is only light, shone through a landscape that is a fine line between this world and whatever else there is around us, before or after.

Heaney did not write these poems for posterity, which is one guarantee of their survival. He wrote them instead for his sometimes anxious, sometimes ailing self, in fortitude against the prospect of no longer being able to write at all. Heaney had similar worries at other times in his career, when he wondered if he would find again the line that pulled him through from one book to another. The debilities of age and sickness were greater again. Faced with them, Heaney called on his old reserves, of place and language, and of his natural inclination to not give in to fear. He is that most remarkable of poets who, like Henry Vaughan, saw the end as light, having worked so long in the dark, a condition Heaney associated with refuge and creativity. Heaney's late poems are literal works of illumination, and it is this, more than anything, that will make a line or poem last, and which gives a reader now a reason, should they need it, to read Heaney now again. There is no end to the dark. Light moves on and shines where it will, as will Heaney's poetry, even in the evening of the world.

Late Heaney. Nicholas Allen, Oxford University Press. © Nicholas Allen 2026.
DOI: 10.1093/9780198985419.003.0006

Further Reading

This portrait of Seamus Heaney and his art proceeded in the first instance from close readings of each of his poetry collections after he won the Nobel Prize: *The Spirit Level* (1996); *Electric Light* (2001); *District and Circle* (2006), and *Human Chain* (2010). This naturally led to reflection on what had come before, and what changed. I explain in the early chapters the social and cultural contexts in which I first encountered Heaney's work, and how it stayed with me. This has included my reading many essays, chapters, and books about his poetry and its contexts. These begin with the collections of his own writing Heaney published in his lifetime, most notably *Finders Keepers: Selected Prose, 1971–2001* (2001), which is an excellent guide to the influence of other poets on his work. In anticipation of an authorized biography, Heaney provided a map of his own past in the interviews he conducted with Dennis O'Driscoll, and which were published as *Stepping Stones* (2009). This guide was given more intimate co-ordinates with the publication of *The Letters of Seamus Heaney* (2023), which, while still partial, gives insight into Heaney's sense of places like Glanmore and the Moyola and of those moments where a word or phrase emerged from consciousness to take shape later in a poem. They also give perspective on his patience and his endurance, both of which qualities speak to the poetic trajectories discussed in this book. The contents of Heaney's personal library are now in possession of the Seamus Heaney HomePlace in Bellaghy.

The classic literary studies of Heaney's early to middle work remain Helen Vendler's *Seamus Heaney* (2000) and Neil Corcoran's *The Poetry of Seamus Heaney: A Reader's Guide* (1986). Andrew Murphy's *Seamus Heaney* (2010) is also a useful guide. Michael Parker's *Seamus Heaney: The Making of the Poet* (1993) is a thorough examination of the contexts of Heaney's writing, a field much expanded by Rosie Lavan's *Seamus Heaney and Society* (2020), which focuses on Heaney's work as an educator and journalist. There are several excellent general studies too, including Heather Clark's *The Ulster Renaissance: Poetry in Belfast (1962–1972)* (2006). Clark's book charts Heaney's navigation of the intense and competitive Belfast literary milieu, which experience no doubt stayed with him for the rest of his writing life, and which explains his sense of freedom after his move to Dublin.

There are essays beyond count on all aspects of Heaney's work across the decades. Two good places to start a general overview are Bernard O'Donoghue's *The Cambridge Companion to Seamus Heaney* (2008) and Geraldine Higgins's *Seamus Heaney in Context* (2021), which contains Brendan Corcoran's helpful essay on 'Poetics', with its glosses on Glanmore, the blackbird, and mourning. My understanding of Glanmore was also enriched by John Dunne's review of the Seamus Heaney HomePlace exhibition in the *Irish Times* of 22 February 2017. Dimitri Hadzi's 'Where in Hellas Was Seamus Heaney' was published in the *Harvard Review* in Spring 1996 and is an invaluable, and warm, account of their travels together, just as Heaney discovered he had won the Nobel. Edward O'Shea's 'Seamus Heaney at Berkeley, 1970–71', published in the *Southern California Quarterly* in 2016, is an excellent guide to Heaney's time in California. Stephen Regan's '*Lux Perpetua*: The Poetry of Seamus Heaney, from *Door into the Dark* to *Electric Light*', published in *Romanticism* 22.3 (2016) was very helpful, as was Michael Putnam's 'Virgil and Heaney: "Route 110"', published in *Arion: A Journal of Humanities and the Classics* 19.3 (Winter 2012). Tara Christie's 'Something to Write Home About': Seamus Heaney at the Hardy Birthplace', published in *The Thomas Hardy Journal* 20.2 (June 2004) is an excellent summary of Heaney's engagements with the English poet to that point. Ronald Schuchard's 'Into the Heartland of the Ordinary': Seamus Heaney, Thomas Hardy, and the Divided Traditions of Modern and Contemporary Poetry', published in *Éire-Ireland* 49 (Winter 2014), was also instructive.

Carmen Bugan's *Seamus Heaney and East European Poetry in Translation* (2013) explained the complexities of a terrain Heaney engaged with closely, and which was a close companion in many late poems. The origins and outlines of Heaney's interest in Milosz are well laid out in Michael Parker's 'Past Master: Czesław Miłosz and His

Impact on the Poetry of Seamus Heaney', *Textual Practice* 27.5 (2013). Parker stresses especially the resonance Milosz's engagement with Catholicism had with Heaney from at least the mid-1970s on. One proposition for the condition of lateness in an artist's life and work is Edward Said's *On Late Style: Music and Literature against the Grain* (2007), as I discuss in a note in the Foreword. The argument for *Late Heaney* is different, but Said's reading has had purchase on the reading of Heaney, principally in R. F. Foster's *On Seamus Heaney* (2020), whose own form as a short study had an influence on this book. A various and sustained account of mortality on Heaney's poetry can be found in *'The Soul Exceeds Its Circumstances': The Later Poetry of Seamus Heaney* (2016), edited by Eugene O'Brien. It is an invaluable complement to this book and a great resource for further study especially of the influences on Heaney's writing. O'Brien is a leading scholar of Heaney in his own right and has published many important essays and books, including *Seamus Heaney as Aesthetic Thinker: A Study of the Prose* (2016). Ian Hickey's *Haunted Heaney: Spectres and the Poetry* (2021) is an insightful guide to the ghostly and gothic aspects of Heaney's writing.

I owe a great deal at several points to *Seamus Heaney and the Classics* (2019), which was edited by Stephen Harrison, Fiona Macintosh, and Helen Eastman. It is full of informative detail and a fascinating read for anyone interested in the register of the classics on contemporary writing. Stephen Harrison and Fiona Macintosh's introduction was very helpful in thinking about Milosz and Sophocles. I owe a particular debt to Rachel Falconer for her observation of the eels' phosphorescence in 'A Lough Neagh Sequence' and the silver foil wrapper in 'Route 110' in her essay 'Heaney and Virgil's Underworld Journey'. Peter McDonald has been consistently one of the sharpest critics of contemporary Irish poetry, and his 'Weird Brightness' and the Riverbank: Seamus Heaney, Virgil, and the Need for Translation' was useful in thinking about *Late Heaney*'s last chapter. These are only two highlights of a book full of insights, brilliantly assembled. *Classics in Post-Colonial Worlds* (2010), edited by Lorna Hardwick and Carol Gillespie, is a further guide to Heaney's poetry in ancient and contemporary contexts, with useful comparison to a diverse range of other writers and experiences. Daniel Donno's essay 'Moral Hydrography: Dante's Rivers', *Modern Language*

Notes 92.1 (January 1977), helped me imagine Heaney's underworld as a water world, a 'hydraulic system' as Donno quotes the critic Charles Singleton.

These works only begin to suggest the depth and diversity of Heaney studies, before we even begin to think about Irish poetry in general, or Heaney's intersections with poets, visual artists, musicians, politicians, and public and private figures from around the world. There are many guides, case studies, and handbooks that can help situate Heaney in these various contexts, most notably *The Cambridge Companion to Modern Irish Poetry* (2003), edited by Matthew Campbell, and *The Oxford Handbook of Modern Irish Poetry* (2012), edited by Fran Brearton and Alan Gillis. There is also a distinguished line of general surveys that relate Heaney's work to various aspects of Irish cultural history, including Terence Brown's *Ireland: A Social and Cultural History* (1985) and Seamus Deane's *Strange Country: Modernity and Nationhood in Irish Writing Since 1790* (1999). I was lucky to be a graduate student of Brown's in Trinity during the late nineties, when I also attended the annual summer schools in Dublin of the University of Notre Dame thanks to Kevin Whelan's kindness. There Deane held us captivated with his dry turns of phrase, his summons of words like a magician. Many of the disputes about Irish literature and culture that followed were published in the pages of little magazines, pamphlets, and newspapers.

There has been much excellent writing about Heaney in the international press over the decades, in the *New York Review of Books* and the *Times Literary Supplement*. The book pages of the *Irish Times* under the editorships of Caroline Walsh, Fintan O'Toole, and Martin Doyle have kept Heaney's writing in conversation with his contemporaries, and with the revival of Irish writing that has flowered in the last decade. Sadly, Caroline passed away before she saw much of the success she helped create, but she is well remembered by the many people she encouraged, myself among them. The literary histories of this moment are still to be written, as is O'Toole's forthcoming biography of Heaney, which will bring together the many threads of the poet's life in one comprehensive study. For a sense of where a literature of critique might turn next, read Darran Anderson's *Inventory: A Memoir* (2020), not least because it shares space with Heaney's Derry, if in a different dimension.

In closing, I am grateful to everyone who has helped me over the years by their conversation and company. I am fortunate to know many brilliant and generous critics, all of whom are in this book, one way or another.

Title Index

For the benefit of digital users, indexed terms that span two pages (e.g., 52–53) may, on occasion, appear on only one of those pages.

Aeneid (translation) 20, 27–8, 83–4, 116, 127–8
'Aerodrome, The' 51–3, 60
'Afterwards' (Hardy) 62–3, 66
'Album' 86–8
'Anahorish' 124
'Antaeus' 57–8
'Anything Can Happen' 121–4
'Apple Orchard, The' (Rilke) 126–8
'Arion' 86
'As the Team's Head-Brass' (Thomas) 55 n.2
'At Toomebridge' 36–7, 124–5
'Audenesque' 70 n.36
'Autumn Journal' (MacNeice) 122

'Bait' 23–4
'Bann Valley Eclogue' 43–5
Beowulf (translation) 27–8, 38–9, 51, 72–4, 83–4, 108–9
'Beyond Sargasso' 22
'Blackbird of Glanmore, The' 29–31
Bloem, J. C. 43
'Bodies and Souls' 96–7
'Bookcase, The' 58–9, 62
'Border Campaign, The' 72–3
'Border Crossing' (Muldoon) 67–8
'Broagh' 124, 128–9

Carson, Ciaran 133
'Casualty' 19–24, 26, 55 n.2
'Chanson d'Aventure' 93–6
'Clonmany to Ahascragh' 126
'Cold Heaven' (Yeats) 6–7
Cure at Troy, The (play) 1, 30, 83–4

'Damson' 97–100
'Digging' 59

'District and Circle' 91–3, 102, 129
'Dog was Crying Tonight in Wicklow Also, A' 114–15

eclogues (Heaney) 43–7, 56–7
Eclogues (Virgil) 43–4, 56–7, 83–4, 127–8
'Ecstasy, The' (Donne) 93–5
'Edward Thomas on the Lagans Road' 54–6
'Eelworks, The' 9–10, 21–2, 25, 92, 112
'Electric Light' 24, 101–3
'Exposure' 11–12, 15 n.36, 38–9, 42, 45, 69, 118

'Feeling into Words' 27–8
'Felix Randal' (Hopkins) 103–4
'Fields of Light, The' 116
'First Words, The' 110–11
'Flight Path, The' 60–4, 66–9, 133
'From the Frontier of Writing' 133–4

'Gathering Mushrooms' (Muldoon) xvii–xviii
'Glanmore Eclogue' 45–7
'Glanmore Sonnets' 4
'Gravel Walks, The' 9–10, 111–15

'Hallaig' (MacLean) 99
'Harvest Bow, The' xvi–xvii
'Herbal, A' 121–2, 126–7
'Home Fires' 70–1
'Human Chain' 15–17, 42, 51, 58–9, 99, 109–10

'In a Field' 55
'Invocation, An' 74–6

'Keeping Going' 135–6
'Kite for Aibhinn, A' 13, 87

144 TITLE INDEX

'Lifting' 25
'Lightenings' 25
'Like as the waves...' (Shakespeare) 6
'Little Canticles of Asturia, The' 47–9
'Loughanure' 48–9, 132–3
'Lough Neagh Sequence, A' 21–4, 26–7

'Main of Light, The' 5
'Mayo Tao, The' (Mahon) 110–11
'Meditations in Time of Civil War' (Yeats) 14
'Meeting Point' (MacNeice) 51–2
'Mid-Term Break' 27 n.19, 82
'Mint' 50–1
'Moyulla' 32–3, 124–5
'Municipal Gallery, The' (Yeats) 14
'Mycenae Lookout, The' 1

'North' xvii–xviii, 24, 42, 112, 116, 120–2, 134–5

'Out of the Bag' 3–4
'Out of this World' 76–9

'Perch' 125–6
'Phosphorescent' 26–7
'Poet's Chair, The' 106–7
'Polish Sleepers' 13, 37–40
'Postscript' 87
Prelude, The (Wordsworth) 16–17, 27–8, 127–8
'Punishment' 120

'Real Names, The' 104–5
'Remembering Malibu' 66
'Requiem' (Akhmatova) 12–13
'Return, The' 26–7
'Rilke: After the Fire' 71–2
'Rilke: The Apple Orchard' 126–8
'Riverbank Field, The' 20, 24, 56, 91–2, 97–8, 127–9, 131–2
'Route 110' 6, 131–3

'Sailing to Byzantium' (Yeats) 76–9, 94–5, 114
'Saw Music (Out of this World)' 76–9
'Scuttle for Dorothy Wordsworth' 70
'Seed Cutters, The' 48
'Seeing the Sick' 103–4
'Setting' 24
'Sharpening Stone, The' 114–15, 117–22
'Shield of Achilles, The' (Auden) 70–1
'Shipping Forecast, The' 26–7
'Sofa in the Forties, A' 36, 90–1
'Sonnets from Hellas' 1–2, 18–20, 33–4
Spirit Level, The 23, 60, 100, 110, 114–15
'Station Island' 19, 37, 42, 47–8, 96
'St Kevin and the Blackbird' 8, 13, 105–6, 119
'Stove Lid for W. H. Auden, A' 70–1
'Strand at Lough Beg, The' 4–5, 55 n.2, 60 n.9, 68, 82–3, 134–5
'Sunlight' 99
Sweeney Astray 46–7, 66, 73–4, 106, 119
'Synge on Aran' 59

'Thistle, the Nettle, The' (Milosz) 38–9
'To a Dutch Potter in Ireland' 40–4
'To Autumn' (Keats) 10–11
'Tollund Man in Springtime, The' 7–8, 28, 41–2, 100–1
'Two Lorries' 88–90

'Up the Shore' 22

'Vision' 26–7

'Walk, The' 114–17
'Westering' 37–8, 58–9, 66–7
'What Passed at Colonus' 79–81
'White Horses' (Kipling) 57
'Whitsun Weddings, The' (Larkin) 91
'Wood Road, The' 36 n.38
'Wordsworth's Skates' 69–70, 121–2
'World, The' (Milosz) 76–7
'Would They Had Stay'd' 76–7

General Index

For the benefit of digital users, indexed terms that span two pages (e.g., 52–53) may, on occasion, appear on only one of those pages.

Ailsa Craig 73–4
Akhmatova, Anna 12–13
Allen, Michael xviii–xix
Antaeus (Greek deity) 57–8
Anthropocene era 33–4
Asclepius (Greek deity) 4
Auden, W. H. xviii–xix, 70–1

Bann River 21, 34–5, 37, 43–5, 50, 124–5
Beckett, Samuel 8–9; as Nobel Laureate 17–18
Bellaghy 15–16
Beowulf 27–8, 38–9, 51, 72–4, 83–4, 108–9
Berryman, John 62 n.16
Bishop, Elizabeth 58
Bloem, J. C. 42–4
Brandes, Rand 65–6
Brodsky, Joseph 70 n.36, 124–5
Brown, George Mackay 74–6
Brown, Sean 2, 19
Bruegel, Pieter 48

Carleton, William 96
Carson, Ciaran 64–6, 133
Chase, William 65–6
Christie, Tara 62
Ciarán, Saint 25 n.12
Clonmacnoise monastery 25
Constable, James 85, 129–30
Cooke, Barrie 27–8, 43–4, 77–9, 85, 94–5

Dante 34, 60, 67–8, 70–1, 90–1, 108
Davidson, Colin 134
Davie, Donald 60
Da Vinci, Leonardo 106–7
Deane, Seamus 123
Donne, John 85–6, 94–5
Douglas, Keith xviii–xix

Elysium 82, 87–8, 106–7, 116, 127–8
environmentalism 32–4

Ferry, David 43–4, 127–8
Field Day 44 n.52, 123
Fitzgerald, Robert 19 n.46, 64–5
Friel, Brian 43–4, 49, 123
Frost, Robert 58

Glanmore 29–31, 66–7
Glob, P. V. 33–4
Gordimer, Nadine 72–3
Grieve, C. M. 74 n.50

Hardy, Thomas 58, 62–3, 66
Heaney, Christopher (brother) 26–7, 82
Heaney, Hugh (brother) 135–6
Heaney, Marie (spouse) 29, 93–5, 114–15, 117, 124–5; father of 117
Heaney, Seamus: at Berkeley 31–2, 63–4; commencement speech of 16–17; death of 131; family of 24, 86–9, 97, 115; at Harvard 64–6; legacy of 131–7; as Nobel Laureate 7–16, 45, 85–6, 111–12; after Nobel Prize xv, 3–4, 14, 16, 126–7; as Oxford Professor of Poetry 29, 64; portraits of 29–30, 134; stroke of 85–6, 93–5, 128–9, 136
Homer 1–2, 14, 64–5, 121–2
Hopkins, Gerard Manley 103–5, 108–9, 115
Horace 67, 121–3
Hughes, Francis 36 n.38
Hughes, Ted 27–8, 47 n.60
Hygeia (Greek deity) 4–5

Joyce, James 19, 37, 61, 96

Kavanagh, Patrick 74 n.50
Kavanagh, Rory 126

Keats, John 10–11, 58
Ker, David 16–17
Kingsmill massacre (1976) 13 n.31
Kipling, Rudyard 57

Landweer, Sonja 27 n.23, 40–4
Larkin, Philip 91, 102, 112–13
Logue, Jim 96
Longley, Michael 58
Loughanure 48–9
Lough Derg 108
Lough Neagh 18, 21–2, 135; ecology of 32–4, 52 n.72; Fishermen's Co-operative of 34–5

MacCaig, Norman 74–6
MacDiarmid, Hugh 58, 74–6
MacLean, Sorley 74–6
MacNeice, Louis xviii–xix, 51–2, 73–4, 122–3
Mahon, Derek 110–11
Mandelstam, Osip 11, 13
McCartney, Colum 2 n.2
McCracken, Mary Ann 58
McElwee, Thomas 36 n.38
McNeill, Mary 58
Middleton, Colin 48–9
Milosz, Czeslaw 9–10, 19 n.46, 27–8, 38–9, 64, 76–81
Milton, John 16–17
Monteith, Charles 18 n.41
Moore, Brian 31–2
Mossbawn 82–3, 111–13
Moyola River 2–3, 18, 23, 27–8, 105, 108–10, 128–9; poem about 32–3, 124–5
Muldoon, Paul xvii–xviii, 58

Nwoga, Donatus 114–15

O'Donoghue, Bernard 29 n.27
O'Driscoll, Denis 14, 136
O'Neill, Louis 2 n.2, 23
Ormsby, Frank xvii

Patrick, Saint 19 n.48, 27, 108–9
Piers Plowman 3–4

pilgrimage 47–8
'prehistorical' 27, 37, 82–3
'purl' 25–6
Pushkin, Alexander 58, 86

Rilke, Rainer Maria 71–2, 126–8

Saddlemyer, Anne 29
Said, Edward xx
Sands, Bobby xvii
Sandymount 31, 48–9, 63–4
Santiago de Compostela 47–9
Schuchard, Ronald 65–6
Shaftesbury, Earl of 34
Shakespeare, William 6, 102, 104–5
Shaw, George Bernard 8–9
Smith, Ian Crichton 74–5
Sophocles 26, 79–81
Spenser, Edmund 102
Stevens, Wallace 58
Stockholm 7–8
Synge, John Millington 15 n.37, 22, 58–9

Thomas, Edward 55–6, 80–1
Toome 34–5, 43–4, 50

Vaughan, Henry 136–7
Vendler, Helen 64–5
Viking raids 38–9, 99, 112
Virgil 25, 43–4, 67–8, 76–7, 82, 85–8, 121–2, 129–30; *Aeneid* 20, 27–8, 83–4, 108–9, 116, 127–8; *Eclogues* 43–4, 56–7, 83–4, 127–8
Vitale, Serena 58

'wood-kerne' 15–16
Wordsworth, Dorothy 70
Wordsworth, William 13, 15–16; *The Prelude* 16–17, 27–8, 127–8
'wound' 97–8

Yeats, William Butler 6, 13–15, 58; as Nobel Laureate 7–9; 'Sailing to Byzantium' 76–9, 94–5, 114; Sophocles and 79–80

The manufacturer's authorised representative in the EU for product safety is Oxford University Press España S.A. of el Parque Empresarial San Fernando de Henares, Avenida de Castilla, 2 – 28830 Madrid (www.oup.es/en or product. safety@oup.com). OUP España S.A. also acts as importer into Spain of products made by the manufacturer.

www.ingramcontent.com/pod-product-compliance
Ingram Content Group UK Ltd.
Pitfield, Milton Keynes, MK11 3LW, UK
UKHW021845020326
468561UK00008B/18/J